Anthology
Volume 2

47 Years Later

With

Russell Atkins

Muntu Dedication

The contributions and remarks from all the surviving Muntu Poets and our mentor Russell Atkins are accepted with much warm appreciation and gratitude; as we embark upon this effort to do a second Anthology, 47 years after our original collection was published in 1968.

Norman Jordan, an acclaimed poet and educator, was a great source of inspiration for the poetry workshop. We want to express warm appreciation and gratitude for the wisdom and the spiritual purpose of his lasting legacy.

Most of the original poets have continued to write and have successfully published in various fields.

We would like to thank Mutawaf Shaheed for coordinating this project, Robert Fleming for his editing expertise, and our publisher K Kelly McElroy for his support.

Page left intentionally blank

The Original Muntu Poets

Russell Atkins
Norman Jordan *

Sababa Akili

Hzal Anubewei (Anthony Fudge)

Yaseen A. Assami (Perry W. Davis)

Sakki Beyti *

Elmer Buford

Robert Fleming

Betty Flannoy *

Marty Freeman *

Omarr Majied *

Art Nixon

Amir Rashidd

Bill Russell

Yahya A. Sabur (Jon Hall)

Mutawaf A. Shaheed (C. E. Shy)

(*) Deceased

Four of the Muntu poets were in the movie *Uptight,*
directed by Jules Dassin.
Russell Atkins, Amir Rashidd, Yahya Sabur, and Mutawaf A. Shaheed.
The movie was made in Cleveland, Ohio 1968.
Shortly after the film was released, the Glenville riots broke out.

Table of Contents

The Original Muntu Poets workshop located on the 2nd floor at the intersection of Ansel Road and Superior Avenue, Cleveland, Ohio. (Photo credit: Yaseen A. Assami)

Introduction

Muntu Poets: Seizing Language, Culture, Souls

"Ignorance, allied with power, is the most ferocious enemy justice can have."

-     James Baldwin (No Name In The Street)

Cleveland, Ohio, the self-described "Mistake By The Lake," was on simmer during the 1960s. The city was segregated with our folks and other unfortunates living in pockets of poverty on its East Side, unable to get valuable jobs in its downtown business district and manufacturing companies, totally shut out of positions at Cleveland Trust, F. W. Woolworth, and Ohio Bell Telephone. Sambo not allowed. With rising rents, low employment, poor schools, and an occupying police force, our young refused to accept "a change was going to come," as the crooner Sam Cooke sang, tossed down the picket signs, and followed the lead of those who revolted in Watts, California in 1965, demanding equality and freedom now.

When the Hough Riots erupted a year later for several days, the Cleveland police force could not put out the rebellion, so the governor called up 2,200 Ohio National Guardsmen to restore order. Word was that a white bar owner, with a hireling, put an inflammatory sign, "No Water For Niggers" at his tavern at E. 79th St and Hough Avenue, with both men standing at the door with shotguns. The locals were outraged and an irate crowd gathered. Cops arrived but were overwhelmed by the firestorm of Black rage. Six nights of arson and sniping against police and guardsmen left four Blacks dead and 30 people critically injured. Several policemen were seriously injured, with 275 arrests and over 240 fires reported.

At the same time, a handpicked state commission blamed the Hough Riots on outsiders, but another panel told the truth: "the underlying causes of the rioting are to be found in the social conditions that exist in the ghetto areas of Cleveland."

More importantly, a federal commission noted that the poverty in Black areas were "the worst they had ever seen." The landlords did little to improve properties and the city fathers limited services to these decaying neighborhoods. There were instances of minor rebellion against the police by the disgruntled locals because they distrusted the corrupted justice by the authorities on their communities.

And then the infamous "Glenville Shootout" happened on July 23, 1968 when the cops and a group of Black men clashed, resulting in an hour of mayhem where four locals and three cops died. A group of Black Nationalists, with Ahmed Evans, attacked the police with shotguns and .30 caliber M-1 carbines, riddling patrol cars and outgunning authorities. This triggered a full-scale revolt with over three days of violence, looting, sniping, and arson.

Enter the Muntu Poets. They reflected the rage, dissent, and rebellious nature of the community during this time. The group consisted of several young members from every political stripe, from liberal to radical, with Hzal Anubewei, Yaseen A. Assami, Sakki Beytu, Norman Jordan, Art Nixon, Sababa Akili, Amir Rashidd, Bill Russell, Yahya A. Sabur, and Mutawaf A. Shaheed. The Muntu Poets, named by Norman Jordan and organized by master poet Russell Atkins, first met at a workshop at Karamu Theatre, one of the oldest theatres in the nation. Later, the group regularly met at a building on Superior Avenue and Ansel Road, where these young men transformed themselves from ordinary citizens to bold literary messengers of defiance and racial pride.

Like any sturdy tree, the Muntu Poets possessed strong roots. One of most significant literary figures in Cleveland, Russell Atkins, a major poet-editor-composer, used revolutionary musical structures in his writing, co-founding possibly the oldest black-owned literary magazine, *Free Lance*, in 1950. He is known as an outlaw of language, experimenting with punctuation, puns, blending textures and colors of words in an abstract concept called "phenomentalism." His poems used colors, moods, events, and verbal magic to full effect. Among his acclaimed works are: *Phenomena (1961), Heretofore (1968), The Nail, to Be Set To Music (1970), Maleficium (1976),* and *Here in The (1976).*

"Russell is the intellect and Norman was the heart and spirit vision," says Hzal Anubewei, whose life was transformed by these two men. "You can't speak of one without the other. They are one body, one concept."

Born in West Virginia and relocating to Cleveland, Norman Jordan was an internationally known poet and playwright. His work has appeared in more than 40 poetry collections, making him one of the most popular voices in the Black Arts Movement. He wrote five books of poetry, including *Destination Ashes, Above Maya, Where Do People In Dreams Come From and Other Poems, Two Books,* and *Sing Me Different.* Ever seeking knowledge, Jordan returned to his hometown, Ansted, in 1977, earning a Bachelor's degree from West Virginia University in theater and a Master's degree in African American studies from Ohio State University. He died in 2015, with many in the literary world mourning his loss.

With the leadership of these two masters, the Muntu Poets embraced the aesthetics of the Black Arts Movement, including poet Larry Neal's concept of "Black Art and Black Liberation:" "Liberation is impossible if we fail to see ourselves in more positive terms. For without a change of vision, we are slaves to the oppressor's ideas and values — ideas and values that finally attack the very core of our existence. Therefore, we must see the world in terms of our own realities."

It was a time of protest, action, and honoring the choice to walk upright and proud. It was a time of Malcolm X, Amiri Baraka, Sonia Sanchez, Nikki Giovanni, the Umbra Poets, the Negritude Poets — Cesaire, Damas, Diop, and Senghor, the Lotus Press in Detroit, Broadside Press and the Third World Press in Chicago. It was the hard-charging juju of the New Music, with high priests such as Coltrane, Albert Ayler, Archie Shepp, Sonny Rollins, Marion Brown, Sun Ra and Cecil Taylor. And the pistol-packing Black Panthers. Spark, rhythm, consciousness.

"We must destroy Faulkner, dick, jane, and other perpetrator s of evil," poet Don L. Lee wrote. "As Frantz Fanon points out: destroy the culture and you destroy the people. This must not happen. Black artists are culture stabilizers, bringing back old values and introducing new ones. Black Art will talk to the people."

The Muntu Poets understood this early on. They wanted to create poems as weapons of culture, poems of illumination and enlightenment, poems that hit hard, poems that sounded the alarm like canaries in coal mines, poems that put the white world on notice.

Mutawaf Shaheed, a poet who found purpose with the group, says: "The voices of dissent were the loudest and it was this group that raised their voices everywhere they went. They were the only group of poets in the city doing that. They felt that everyone else was putting honey and perfume on shit."

"I do believe that we were called together to do a very important and great thing by some unknown force or forces in our lives," recalls

Yaseen A. Assami, a Muntu member. "Us being in Muntu was a part of that calling. There were no other group of any kind, just us and our dreams STRAIGHT NO CHASER."

The elder of the group, Elmer Buford, remembers other literary groups in Cleveland largely ignored them, but the college circuit and progressive churches welcomed them such as Buffalo State University and Antioch College. While some of the others embraced the heated rhetoric of the Black Arts Movement, he patterned his work on the Harlem truth-teller, James Baldwin, probing the deeper cultural and social issues of the community.

"The Muntu Poetry Workshop has to be viewed in the context of being a united front collective of artists, meaning that the group didn't impose any political or religious views on its members," Sababa Akili says. "Some of us were community organizers, working to empower our people. We worked with young people in the schools, lectured on college campuses, advocated for Black Studies, for cultural awareness and political empowerment."

The last Muntu meeting occurred on July 23, 1968, the same date of the Glenville shoot-out.

To close this fitting tribute to Russell Atkins, Norman Jordan and the Muntu Poets, the vanguard of local revolutionary black arts movement in Cleveland, Art Nixon summed it up: "We were going to change the world, using words and ideas to do it. We realized the power of language to fire up the mind and spark action. We wanted to change awareness and stop our community from the status quo."

Yes, the Muntu Poets are older but wiser. Their words still resonate in these troubled times - riveting, passionate, and provocative. This anthology of our esteemed poets-magicians is a powerful tonic for the mind and soul. Enjoy!

Robert Fleming, New York City, December, 2015

Russell Atkins

Russell Atkins (Photo credit: Diane Kendig)

Russell Atkins

(Photo credit: Charles Pinkney, charlespinkney.com)

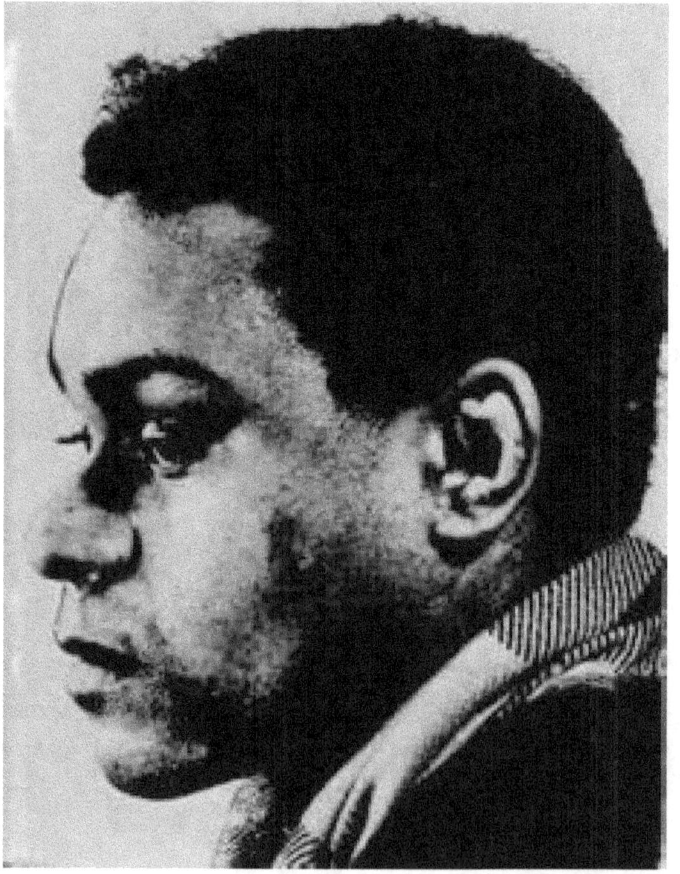

DAWN (Rest Home)

a hag'd like laughter
laughter that hags

now and then
down the hall
more laughed hag'd

thither of lit
is of a room thus'd to odd
with about shadow'd
    a door's nearby of at
    of/in, or/out, or/of, a door's from
COLD OPEN
    on somewhere

    aloud voices{ Next:
GOOD morning, good morning,}
    GOOD morning, sir,
GOOD morning all,
        (Good (Oh Really?
          Who says so?
beheld as day "dares" up to up'd
    then falls
        to eve'd
meanwhile
then and now
hag'd laugh

Written by Russell Atkins August, 2015

Russell Atkins
HERE IN THE

CLEVELAND STATE UNIVERSITY
POETRY CENTER

EVENING REELECTIONS IN A BIRDBATH

still   there in our birdbath
strangely eye like   light
repeated from the sky
ill of it there is the   so small
touch of a world's beware

some leafy shadows overs
from trees wind swell'd
the yard commonoplaces
now
          household sentiments,
                    a rake, the lawnmower

until more stark than ever
in the round of the bowl
the always terror
stares out
          and out
          with a *lo!*

Objects
Russell
Atkins

FLU AS A OLD WAR MOVIE

They're *the* strategists! They first clamp
Off the food supply from the port:
Heavy gunfire around the gut warehouse,
Like guards stabbed, one whipped cold
                    With a gun butt.

They seize the camouflaged brain radio
Scrambling the signals. Anyway, signals
Can't get through.   With flame throwers
They close in and in and tight.

While brain waves burn, a crack
Lung Team hits at breath.   They reconnoiter
Spraying the lobar regions - cold gook
From their Chemico-Warfare Division!

They've got one objective: the big
Muscle Center whose dynamos -
        huge pericardium masses – thunder
                  until whack,
        light is zapped, electricity's
out –
        something it out!

Objects 2 authored by Russell Atkins

NEW STOREFRONT

Afresh'd with paint, the shop had glare:
chrome-plated the squared of for sale,
angles, or with glamorous rounds.
                    Auto Supply Co.
The owner looked too outright
(dart of a much refracted stare).
Aluminum hat set him blind awhile –
the false going virtue of hope

no public interest anywhere about

his innocence   among the smokeshops
the parlors of the barbeque, the bars
and barbershops proliferous.   All these
dives without sheen and more secret,
sinfully wised, merely glimmered

he dared their margins with silver

Russell Atkins on the cover of *The Chesnutt Record*
(Photo credit: Charles Pinkney, charlespinkney.com)

OUT OF JOINT

not with his wife at eased
on the refresh of his front porch?
        not painting about
the house? not tying up the dog
with a wave of responsibility?
not watering his lawn?

but out here with
pieces of red aglow, leer, on
the creased pavements, boozed over:
        sleazsys of nightclubs
and not of our neighborly path

        he furtives by
unnoticing   urged to a prowl,
gargoyled with desires:
        his companion
unseeming   as a relative
unseeming   even as of old friends
        or of a family
that visits after church

        they furtive beyond
talking of "bitches"
talking of "ass"

Russell Atkins with members of the Writers Workshop (John
Donoghue, Bob Donoghue, John Stickneyam, and Faheem Khabeer
(sitting far left)); and some members of the Original Muntu Poets
including: Norman Jordan (standing 2nd from left), Mutawaf Shaheed
(standing 4th from left), Yaseen A. Assami (standing last from left), and
Yahya Sabur (sitting last from left)
(Photo credit: Diane Kendig)

SHIPWRECK

With today's sympathetics who can be
                              dare?
in the old days when sailed struck,
sank, who knew?   few, comparatively
(- no speaking cabinets,
much less "typographical" compassion)
But these days terroring,
the grim fashion's that the speaking cabinet
and typographical
leave what sympathetics more than fear?
— dawn sheds appear'
on broken, strewn, muted in oil and algae
sarcastic'd to a shore — ducks death,
fish death; the senses ewven
aver the air's dark-ages' legions;
                    - sheep,
too, strange away, dying:
midnight trains farewell of track
stealth back with deadly loads;
                    - woe-ing
its worst all yesterday,
a multitudinous famine!

(as for long life and as for love?
list with the undertaker, thrumming
numb, undering through the hush
— what is more shipsunk wept for?)

be dare sympathize —

                   even if it is

unwise?

Russell Atkins with Faheem Khabeer
(Photo credit: Diane Kendig)

THE LOST SCARF

A cursing thunder of gloom came across from
     then an hysteria of rain after.
Up from below, a shuddering gigantic surge!
The stark wrapped up whole of an evening of the fall.
I wore a dirtied, restless'd scarf (sentiment, though,
     loved it).
Wind reaching out of that garden of forever –
     that half of hollow'd of the fall –
     got it and shredded it, spectred it through
     the hideous blur; agonized it on the dead,
     rustled lawn, tortured it against, convolved it with!
It then disappeared by the tomb of the Rhones!
It had hung among souvenirs, lately been of occasions
     (the memories of which I was fond).
I sought it, the loved, over, about, beside
     Soft, treaded the coffins

The Chesnutt Record feature article with Russell Atkins shown with Hale Smith, conductor and composer
(Photo credit: Charles Pinkney, charlespinkney.com)

TRAINYARD AT NIGHT

TH UN DER   TH UN DER
the huge bold blasts black
hiss insists upon hissing insists
on insisting on hissing insists
hiss s sss ss sss sss ssss s
ss sssss ssss
when whoosh!
the sharp scrap making its fourth lap
with a lot of rattletrap
and slap rap and crap –
I listen in time to hear coming on
the great Limited
it rolls scrolls of fold of fold
like one traditionally old
coldly, meanwhile hiss hiss
hiss insists upon hissing hiss
hiss s ss ss sss sss s
sss s s
s

Russell Atkins: The man and His Work

(Continued from page 10)

In 1976 Cleveland State University presented an honorary degree to Russell Atkins words: " A lifelong Cleveland resident you have written of its social foibles and graces, its natural beauty and the hopes of its people."

When Daniel R. Biddle wrote the Plain Dealer article of June 13, 1976 he referred to Atkins as "one of Clevelad's greatest living poets". There can be little question that Russell Atkins has contributed to the literary, musical and theoretical tradition of both disciplines, not only locally but nationally and internationally.

In concluding his biographical sketch of Atkins in the Dictionary of Literary Biography, Ronald Henry High says, "Finally, as more people get familiar with Atkins, his approach to literary expression will be better appreciated and more understood. As his work is more performed and more read, as it garners more critical attention and documentation his genius will come to be recognized in the United States as it is in Europe.

My own experience in doing the research and interviews for this profile have left me with one unalterable impression of the man and his work: Russell Atkins is a living Treasure. The discovery of his rich theoretical base for what on first sight seems incomprehensible is rendered intelligible when measured against the philosophical soundness of his theories and work.

Consider for an example Atkins assertion that music and composition are separate entities. During the 1950's Atkins advanced a theory of music which he termed **psychovisualism** (published in Free Lance 1955-1956-1958) The theory incorporates elements of Gestalt Theory with its notion of forming of complex yet specific recognizable patterns. Atkins argues that the brain not the ear is the right instrument for understanding composition in music. The ear he attests is merely the receiver of stimuli. Stefan Wolpe introduced the concept at the Darmsadt Festival of Contemporary Music in 1956.

In his book Twentieth Century Music 1969 European music critic   H. H. Stuckenschmidt gave credit to Atkins as having influenced the musical Avant-garde centers of Europe.

Inevitably the question of why/how could this "genius" whose many literary and musical credits which will be the subject of part II of the profile - have passed into a shadow of obscurity. This man whose chamber works have been performed by members of the Cleveland Orchestra..this man who has collaborated with Langston Hughes and Robert Shaw Chorale in the production on "In Memoriam" by Cleveland Composer/ Conductor Hale Smith...this man who broke the starchy poetic construction of his day and survived the dogged insistencies to pigeonhole and reduce his work and theories into some academic mutant. One is left to speculate about such oversights - or perhaps more correctly injustices of those who select the "important contemporary writers" Russell Atkins Rightly Belongs at the Head of the list.

Note: *The author is the founder and Executive Vice President of the Charles W. Chesnutt Literary Society.*

HOMELESS

By Russell Atkins

His less barber'd hair vagabonds

as of more slept

too much in parks:

old friends would flee

him if they glimpsed

how far his veer

from sprawled houses

that flaunt their lavish,

from golf courts, Jaguars,

cocktail parties

he's somebody yore,

flunk'd of fortune

-- but a bag now

folded to shred!

he may despond

to a lake's like a sea

that's luminous but not of cheer

and gives a bath

-- then sleep

Part of the feature article with Russell Atkins in *The Chesnutt Record*
(Photo credit: Charles Pinkney, charlespinkney.com)

34

WORLD'D TOO MUCH (IRRITABLE SONG)

Buss hollows on   of back windows
awidth'd where oxygen, gust'd,
crosswise of neglect, a joyous'd
foregone of seats, the while a beer can's
joust'd about the floor's rubbish'd
and a driver's on the last run
as of fatal'd alone –
            how such cheerfuls me!
then someone boards
            there's always somebody

            Once, wood'd,
(hazed by a dell's emerald'd,
that is, pastel's from a green rain)
aloned hush had banished heard,
no one for hours! Perfect, I thought,
such Gatbo! – until
I saw someone afar'd, somebody by
- again

Cloister of a libray's mum,
the half mute books rigid'd
with what's ceased, held;
and worlds-away of noise was thrill
as shunned   when eh!
Another entered   sat
(- and wouldn't you know -)
somebody *always*

        Even in dreamt
yons from a shores'd escape,
silent'd in a moon's sequin'd shining
in a rowboat's bask

Russell Atkins with lady poets and Dr. Bruscella Jordan (left to right):
Zena Zipporah, Diane Kendig, Dr. Bruscella Jordan, and Sharan Paul
(Submitted by Mutawaf Shaheed)

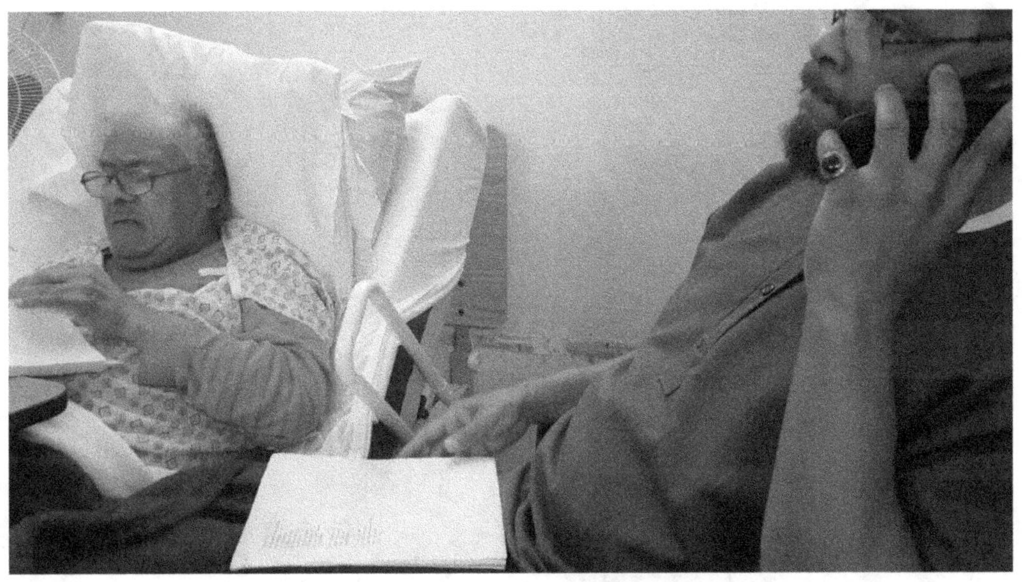

Russell Atkins with Original Muntu Poet Mutawaf Shaheed
(Photo credit: K Kelly McElroy)

Norman Jordan *

Feeding the Lions

They come into
our neighborhood
with the sun
an army of
social workers
carrying briefcases
filled with lies
and stupid grins

passing out relief
checks
and food stamps
hustling from one
apartment to another
so they can fill
their quota
and get back out
before dark.

Where Do People In
Dreams Come From?
& Other Poems
Norman Jordan

I Have Seen Them

I have seen them trying
to sober up
to be heard
to listen
to live
Lord Knows, I have seen them.

I have seen them waiting
for relief
for a job
for winter to pass
for life
Yes Lord, I have seen them.

I have seen them crying
because it's too late
because they can't feed their babies
because they are tired of maybe
because they are afraid
Dear Lord yes, I have seen them
Praying
For miracles.

Copyrighted Material
NORMAN JORDAN
SING ME DIFFERENT
New & Selected Poems by
Copyrighted Material

Kuumba

Life is
Creative force
In motion
MOVE!!!

Norman Jordan with Theresa Burriss, Contributing and Senior Editor of *PLUCK :The Journal of Afrilachian Arts & Culture,* and Ken Heckler, former West Virginia Congressman at West Virginia Library Commission event

One For All

What we
Give
Our children
Let us
Envision
It be given
To all children

What we
Desire
Let us
Desire
For our
Sisters and brothers also

Let us be brothers and sisters
And
Mothers and fathers
Of each
Other
And let not
One of us be
Brotherless or sisterless
Or
Motherless or fatherless

Let us
Eat
Sleep and live
As one
And
If a person
Comes to bless

Or hurt me
Let them
Meet
Us all.

Poet Norman Jordan and Poet James Cherry

Popsicle Cold

Now
that the story
has moved
out of the headlines
the widow
of the dead black hero
stands alone
at the public market
purchasing polluted pork
with government
food stamps

Norman and Dr. Brucella Jordan

The White Prophecy

Scream you wise men
of bacteria.
Scatter your pamphlets
and prophecy.
Place your statues
on every corner.
Scream until your tonsils
dry up like used teabags.
Scream to every idiot
that will tolerate you.
Preach your tired, timid ideas.
Scream, scream, scream!
Make them believe in your
sick holy word.
Make them believe in
Your evil death.
Make them soldiers in
your ignorant army.
MAKE ME PUKE!

Sababa Akili

A poem for women who have
written
poems to themselves

(hum) you abandoned me.......love

don't live here any more

A poem for women who have

written poems to themselves

about

life, about love and

lovers (some distant now)

about children,

about difficulties, about pain

about loneliness and all sorts of thangs

For our sisters

beautiful women who have struggled

cried, laughed,

loved and had dreams murdered.

For you women

In your pants, skirts, sun dresses and lapas

heads fro-ed or fried

For you sisters who have suffered but never died

For Ms. fine minded beautiful ladies (looking at me right now)

For your tears, for your fears

For all those years

For the Rubys, Dorothys, Billies, Ethels, Sewas, and Ayanas

For the Annies and Fannies, Assattas, Jessica and Glorias (for whatever

your mama

named you)

or (you named yourselves)

The Muntu Poets

This is a poem for your mind
For you to love in the midnight hour
When your toes tickle the darkness
And sweat rains down
On your Mr. Melody as you do the do (beauty)
For the cold mornings
and empty memories
For the brick like tears that fall
leaving faces disfigured
For you beautiful women
who have endured and given
but refused to be driven
For you my sisters
for the trips and the games and the
lovers without names
wait
what could be more beautiful
than a black woman loving and
being love (absolutely nothing)
or when she's blue / and blue black
strains of pain rains from shattered hearts
or when sun lit laughter fills the room
crushing the coldness of American madness
beautiful eyes whispering brother let's struggle
and our enemies grimace at your persistence
cause in you / a new world is born each time you smile
in you / from this seed
comes a child
For these women, these sisters
For the young and old
For these women of soul

we hear you moaning sister
in empty rooms
sweet beauty and pain
we love you
we love you
we love you / yes we do
So new world sisters of ancient beauty
Magical ladies
Stretch out in this world and become, be coming
be coming, be coming
when the world thought you were going
Keep on coming, honey, sister, baby,
baddest creature on the planet, lady
be coming out for love
for struggle
for victory
cause you bad / yeah, you bad,
and we love you
yeah, we love you / yes we do!   **sababa akili / 2001**

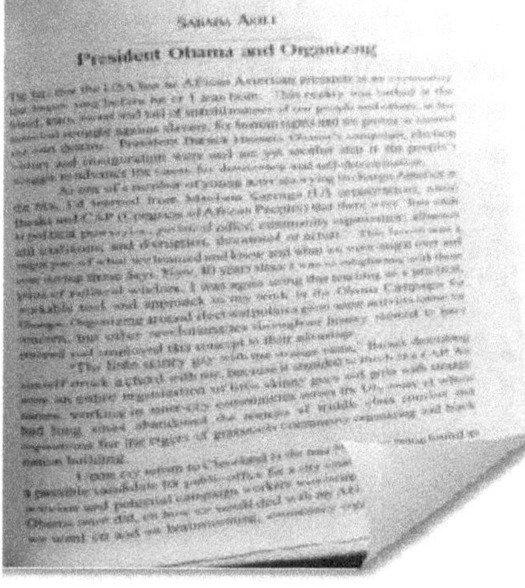

Sababa Akili is a contributing writer in these anthologies

Aint no mother like a real mother for you

(A Poem for Amina Baraka)

Wear the crown, the title –
For us it has nothing to do with stale ass aristocratic women,
dingbats of capital that live off the toil of their minions
First mother of Newark, this is who we see you as,
and who you were long before Ras was born/became mayor.
You are, the first mother of Newark because you are and were,
for the many of us from the various places throughout this place called
usa.
Drawn to Newark, to give of our minds and muscles
for a mission about our liberation.
You were for many of us our new mother,
maybe for some the only mother known.
Educating, feeding, and nurturing the masses of us
after furious days of work and struggle.
You gave order and social order to our lives
within the matrix of this madness.
You counseled souls, was even called mother Amina,
not because you desired to be called such, but because that is who
you were
and what you did.
The masses of us were your children,
alongside your biological children
who became our sisters and brothers.
We cared for them like you cared for us,
We became the biggest family in this city, in this nation.
And the masses of Newark witnessed this,

perhaps not understanding until now that one of your children
leads the city and when he became Mayor, they became Mayor.
Now they seek to give recognition to the fact
that you always were and will be the first mother of Newark,
because no other mother in its history has had more children than
you,
No other mother in its history has given as much,
nourished so many, help orchestrate the weddings of so many of your
daughters,
kept an eye on so many of their houses.
Planned and organized and mobilized, and oversaw the well-being,
of all these children who became men and women right before your
very eyes.
Some went on to bring gladness to your heart, some perhaps only
sadness.
What's a mother to do?
In our struggle for self-determination,
the people endeavor to define and name for themselves
and if they believe you are the real mother of their city
under the leadership of your child.
There is enough history and struggle to back them up!
Black Lives Matter!

s.akili/2015

My Brother Amiri B

A mouth full of lyrics
so clear – you could see his truth
from here to the sun
vocal cords, rapid firing like AK's
words of truth coming forth to enlighten
your ass, if that's what you need
to burn your ass if you be any
kind of assorted oppressor
you think cause he's gone you can rejoice?
not so fast you shit carriers of this capitalist doodoo
because we still have poems
that choke neanderthals
and tom-ass clarences,
poems that shoot guns
and yes, poems that kill our tormentors
Black Lives Matter!

sababa akili / 2015

Original Muntu Poets including (left to right): Amir Rashidd, Sababa Akili, Bill Russell, Mutawaf Shaheed, and Yahya Sabur performing at League Park Center

The Soul

The boat is empty
drifting aimlessly,
riding the gentle
ripples of this river
The sun rays glances
artistically, off the
ebb and flow of the water
There is no steward present,
the captain has gone
The boat is empty
untethered, unfettered,
free to go wherever
Like a soul
freed of its old captain,
and earthly catchings
It may ride the
currents of the wind
skyward
Some may say
heaven bound,
but to ascribe a
destination, would be
To tether it again
to the limits of
our earthly imagination
and knowledge

sababa akili / 2007

Original Muntu Poets (left to right): Mutawaf Shaheed, Sababa Akili, Norman Jordan, and Bill Russell after a poetry reading for the Cleveland Ethical Society

This Ain't TV

As the world turns
and crosses burn
Now jellybeans instead of peanuts
and old western movies
are being shown in the White House
Cartoon senility grins
and waves from the balcony
As Nixon's sings push, push,
Push him Bush
the skeletal remains of j edgar nods
with approval
It is another world and all the days of our lives
we see this madness hurled against us
Flash – Greensboro
Flash - Grenada
Flash – No Goode Wilson in Philly
Flash – Flash - Atlanta
It is cold blooded murder
Yet resistance comes from
the young and the restless
as the search for tomorrow continues
The omnipotence of the rulers
the super nonsense
of the cracker world hangs
against the consciousness
of the people
Straight out of comic land
With bullets and death a super cracker
with an "s" on his chest

the mighty whore in her invisible plane
a jungle punk, his monkey and jane
But this is not TV
This is the real world
No bionic boys or bionic girls
no incredible hulk or spider and buck
No mystical heores
nor uncle tomming neegroes
will save you America
So come on with the klan
it's your only shot
and the streets in this country will burn
red hot
Cause sheets burn like crosses on American bosses
and flaming racist asses will light up the sky
as any winter becomes hotter than july

sababa akili / 1986

Original Muntu Poet Workshop located on the 2nd floor at the intersection of Ansel Road and Superior Avenue in Cleveland, Ohio (Photo credit: Mutawaf Shaheed)

Hzal Anubewei (Anthony Fudge)

Father

I am the father

who was the son

My

day is upon me.

In my hands are the obligations

the working tools of manhood passed on to me.

Just before sunrise I meditate

HaHiYa speak wisdom to me.

When my wife looks at me let love shine

When my children call

let a smile be on their face

I am the father

who was the son.

Now

I am a citizen

son of my people son of a nation

I carry iron the work men must do

I pray for the fathers that fight to keep us free

The word love beats on my chest

Across my shoulders is a harness

like my father I must learn to pull my weight

Carry the water of life

until my days are done

Embracing both sorrow and joy

arms on the same body

at night just after moonrise

I gather my family

hold them for just a little while

tell them what I know of wisdom

The Muntu Poets

I am the father
who once was the child
I am the father
who was the son

The Muntu Poets

I am the father
who was the son

Go

When
religions stop saying words men understand
then men stop speaking to religions
spending time on their stomachs
none on their knees
raising items that smoke to their lips
GO
no hand signals used in ceremonies
obeying none of the traffic shuffling to and from holy doors
expensive buildings granite and marble mansions
of many rooms
great auditoriums housing the poor of pocket
the effects of society grim
the world chewing on the grains of war
the martyrs blood everywhere
look at the eyes of the babies
the little girls and the little boys
GO.
is it crime
that we want these wonderful minds to absorb
even the trees have turned their backs
the misery explodes into fires
burning across the plains
huge water spouts rush across the oceans
to put out the flames
men have created
religions spew out the generation across the lands
silver symbols and gold lockets
they sing in the aisle

sending up prayers for victory
blessing soldiers against one another for the nation
we hope love still lives
we hope that the angels still believe
there is hope for men
we hope that god will forgive us
every book of wisdom speaks of death
its rights and its wrongs
none celebrate death   all seek its mercy
all wait for the day when the hands of the other world
reach across
lift us into that place beyond our knowing
GO.
how do we tell the babies
about the blood on our hands
the scenes of death and destruction
we instruct for grace and the will of god
we carry a knife behind our back
to slice away pieces of our children's eyes
we cut into the heart of goodness
and plant flowers and light candles
in the graveyards of the soldiers of war
will we take
pieces of our children's eyes into heaven tomorrow
will we carry
remains of the heart of goodness into heaven
will we come
with knives and weapons
of death   of destruction
will we speak from the graveyards
forgive us

GO.
how do we follow leaders that give orders
to kill other men   other women
the babies of another nation
bleeding in beds instead of sleeping
the priests said it was ok
making religion a national banner
conspiring against
what the prophets said
no man should do
according to the words of holiness
GO.
where are the bright mornings
where are the peaceful evenings of sunsets
I have looked for the fields of green hearts
I have found sacrifice and blood
not of the lamb nothing of the fish
the moon sits in the sky
on her throne anchored in space
toss up the names of the valiant heroes
stars composing scenes of the trails of men
metal caravans and wagon trains
natives on the trail of tears
on and on into the fog of time
into the mist of mystery
every moment before us
becomes the next great mountain
hills of struggle and runaway valleys
can we know peace in this generation or the next
we keep moving
replacing one dream with another

faces coming out of the water to speak truth
leaking from every pore
an explosive mixture of fiery lies and billowy truths
all different when the sun comes again

GO.
one day with another
even if we tried to let go we couldn't
because go has a hold of us
go and be a child
go and grow up
go run
go fly
go be still
go destroy
go rebuild
go break a heart
go make love
go and forgive
go and meditate
go and be peaceful
go go go go go go

Pouring Shade

Pour
some shade on the road
to cool my feet
pour some on my hands
tired from the week
pour some sweet shade on my head
I need some relief
Let it flow like honey
      drip like maple syrup
serve me a glass of lemonade
stirred to the taste of sweet shade
Pour it over everything
Pour it on a rainbow
Even
the colors of nature want to know
how it feels to taste sweet

PROSE WITH A TWIST

A
SCHEME
IN EVERY
SCENE

HZAL ANUBEWEI FUDGE

PRODUCTION
SCENE
TAKE
DIRECTOR
CAMERA
DATE

Smoke on the Ground

I see a wasteland of bodies without heads
a generation disconnected from their ancestors
their heads split into degrees of pain and suffering
Released from broken buildings
words of fire escape
the sound of hip hop ripped from heads
floating in the hood
the nation of a brown skin people
whose child is missing
Angels fly on human rockets searching for souls
burning bodies just smoke on the ground
run into tomorrow
looking at yesterday
alive next door
the cycle of misery a treadmill that goes on and on
changing the song by switching the words
symphony's of discord grind on street corners
backed by the horns of gunshots
the syncopation of the rape of a nation
the blood of passing made by holes in the back
lying men bring flowers smoking from gunfire
let me be the one who says it is time for us to stop
let me be the first one
and the last one to say I'm sorry
 let me be the one
looking in the eyes of the brown nation
say joy has replaced sadness
 say that the missing child
the messenger of hope is coming home

a full grown man
the moment of healing
resurrected ashes of burning bodies
smoke on the ground rises
evaporated by the light of the sun
ancestor receive us
sing songs we haven't heard before
the Cry of Beauty in a city of peace

The Poet

If it were just a simple story
I would have told you so.
It is a more involved idea.
You don't know how I want to be the Poet
Not the truck driver
Not the politician
Not the sky or the stars
Not the guarantee
I want to be the Poet
I would reveal the poetry of life
It has gone out of this world
I would create an endless well of images
To drown the world in joy
And make tears a separate thing
I would bid each voice to sing
I am the Poet
and
must be other things as well
But when it comes
The dying time
By what name will the people know me
If not
The Poet
If it were a simple story
I would have told you so
More in the telling
More in the deed

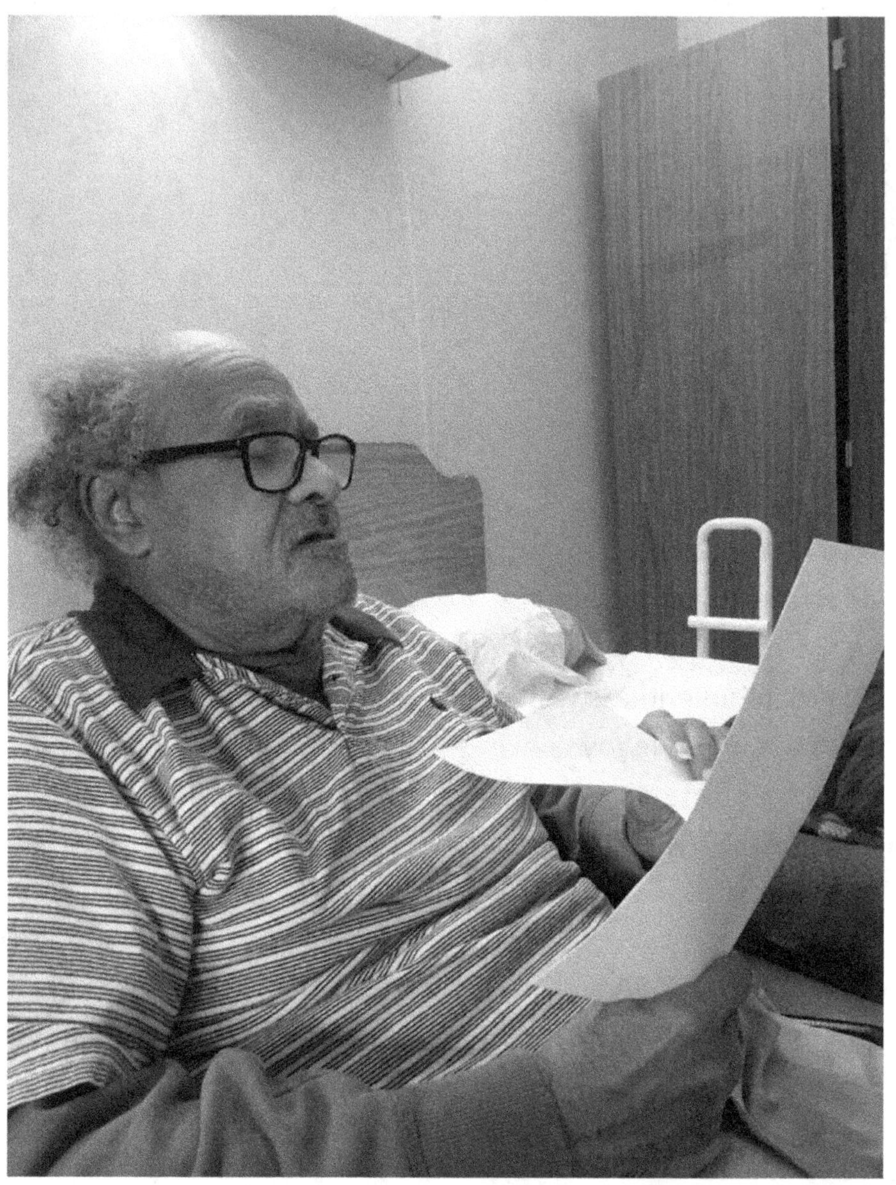

Russell Atkins reviews recent poetry By Muntu Poet Mutawaf Shaheed
(Photo credit: Mutawaf Shaheed 2015)

Weight of a New Season

words bend over the wind

the weight of a new season

steel wheels roll the train

trees slip backward past time moments ago

Arla and Ankey arms on seats

the window presents the cast

citizen crowded sidewalks   crowded buildings thick

houses exercising paint   brush aside past deeds

large manicured stones corner upscale markets

landscaped cows and pastures venture out

fat flowers rush to catch sunlight

the large sound of open country

Arla and Ankey exchange eyes

they bend words over the space between them

they are ornaments glistening skin

Arla pulls the lips of Ankey

Ankey slips on the feet of Arla

night quickens a dark shadow

legs crouch in an eight hour huddle

On the noon of noon the next day

words lean over the wind

the weight of a new season

steel wheels kill the train

Arla and Ankey unwarm the seats

the window cast them out

trees announce their presence moving their limbs

citizens language speaks a familiar tongue

rooflines rims remind a remembrance neighbors past

slow steps quickly pass a hardware

The Muntu Poets

the merry café   rich Peter's grocery
so many hands touched
so many cheeks buried together
happiness unchecked outside
one comes   his innards distilled   dripping danger
falling for years
an arrow of hate in a lunge in a crowd
Ankey and Arla wounded under the soul
nightgowns in the hospital
spotlight of the news
Arla and Ankey arms on beds
steel bullets close to the kill
newspaper clippings locked away in yellowing boxes
retreating to fire the new chimney
come skin slip in
let us mend the wind with words
let us lift the weight of a new season
the space between us retreating
we collide without nightgowns
crashing our ornaments
slipping on feet and pulling lips
crouching in an eight hour huddle of passion
the wind lies on its side
the weight of a new season bends the horizon
our horses stand at attention pawing the ground
our necks turning surveying the rooflines of new neighbors
smoke circling into a cloud above our new home
a quiet choir of restless trees
 memories drifting through weakened heads
Years in the days long ago
ghostly faces full of dread

Omarr Majied, one of the Original Muntu Poets (in rear with firearm), with Cleveland Mayor Carl Stokes (Submitted by Marcus Greenwood)

Yaseen A. Assami (Perry W. Davis)

Yaseen A. Assami (Perry W. Davis)

A Late Summer's Night Goodbye

The end has come to narrow the space between your heart and my
dream
Tyme will heal the wanderings of a heartache.
Soothing the moments we never had
Looking past answers to a place filled with goodbyes and
never more
We can feel
We cry
We desire
Each embrace pushes us past needs and closer to a passion that
lives
Within a vison of love.
Empty space
Empty eyes
Empty minds
Empty people die Empty
Leaving grave yards filled with tears and disparity.
No questions ask .
No meaning to give,only the slow melting away of a connection made
When the balance between pain and joy was poised on a tear.
No need to go
No need to remember
Only the need to understand,Where should i go from here?
For now? Are should i go, away?
And let now never happen

Again? Wishing you the best not knowing what that means,hoping to
see you one more tyme
Knowing it might be to late to catch the star lite in your eyes
To little
Too late
To bad
To few
To too many empty moments and lost dreams.?

Yaseen A. Assami 11/29/2015......?

Microwave Grits

Sitting here in the dark surrounded by four corners of a place life has carved from the bitter sweet past of some halfhearted effort to be free from the precautions of a broken man's effort to understand the needs of the many or the nigger next door.

Listing to the cold winter wind whisper the blues about the coming of spring and tapping a tune about the last storm on a melting snowflake.

Searching for a soft place to land and watching life creep away in the shadows of a forgotten lullaby.

Remembering the song mother sang as she faded away into a place surrounded by hope and desperation

Watching father turn small chances into major provisions as he rehearsed the hopes and dreams of john Coltrane, McKinley Morganfield and Emit Teal.

Waiting for the sun to rise while the roar of a tear etches fond memories of yesterday on tomorrow's goodbye.

Yaseen AsSami

08/25/2013

Publication Pending. Uptown Media Joint Ventures

Mister Same Thang 2 mr. will #3

Standing in some empty alley holding a basket full of hope, waiting for a truck load of trouble, watching the tear stained meaning of an empty promise turn to poison Mr. Same Thang caresses temptation with a hopeful hand and a wishful smile.

One day closer to a sorrowful meeting of two empty souls, he hears the wind called Maria whisper Mary. Lost ambitions and broken promises leave Mr. Same Thang   restless and lonely. Mr. Same Thang Works his way past a blues song sung by a drunken bumblebee and hears maggots gossip about the distance between deaths and decay, funky tired and defeated Mr. Same Thang

 Crawls along 7 mile hills with 10% grades counting the distance between pessimistic days and satisfactory beginnings, the blues echoes across the back of his head scaring his mind with the emotions of a time when his experiences painted a picture of success.

Well-dressed soothsayers fill his pockets with the wishes of Wall Street junkies and past the hopes and dreams of his children with a Frankenstein hero.

Life leaves Mr. Same Thang in disbelief as his flesh shrinks with age. gray hair; stiff knees, slow reflexes, and short breath giving the way to wisdom understanding and deliberate actions. The music changes and so does the flow of the ink between the pen and the word. Mr. Same Thang sits wondering can john lee hooker sing the blues.

His eyes dance along the pages of life wondering how far he is from the answers to the questions asks by a thousand empty eyed broken hearts and forgotten memories of lost love.

A phase between fall and winter carves a image of spring on the face of October causing a smile and a tear and Mr. Same Thang stumbles and drops dead in a pile of snow.

Original Muntu Poet, Mutawaf Shaheed, at 3RD Annual Cuyahoga County Public Library poetry reading. Now a present member of one of the "oldest" poetry workshops in the United States.
(Photo credit: Yaseen Assami)

Putting a Twenty on a Ten

Guns blazing lights flashing children screaming

Junebug crying

What you doing Billy???

He say . I be puttin a 20 on a10.

Dumb negros everywhere.

Scraping the last remains of a lullaby forgotten

Off the bottom of a Blues opera

Humming the star spangle banner and whispering lies

About the trials and troubles

Of Jesus The Christ

Spitting into the wind and and caressing sorrows

What you doing.?.

Junebug!!Billy!

They say we be puttin twenty on ten

Clang clang

Buzz buz

Zip wiz rumble young man rumble

I stand here in the middle 0f nowhere

Being restricted by someone tring to get to a place where

The Muntu Poets

All things are umlimited

Bang Bang Bang

What the Hell??? Putting A 20 on A 10.

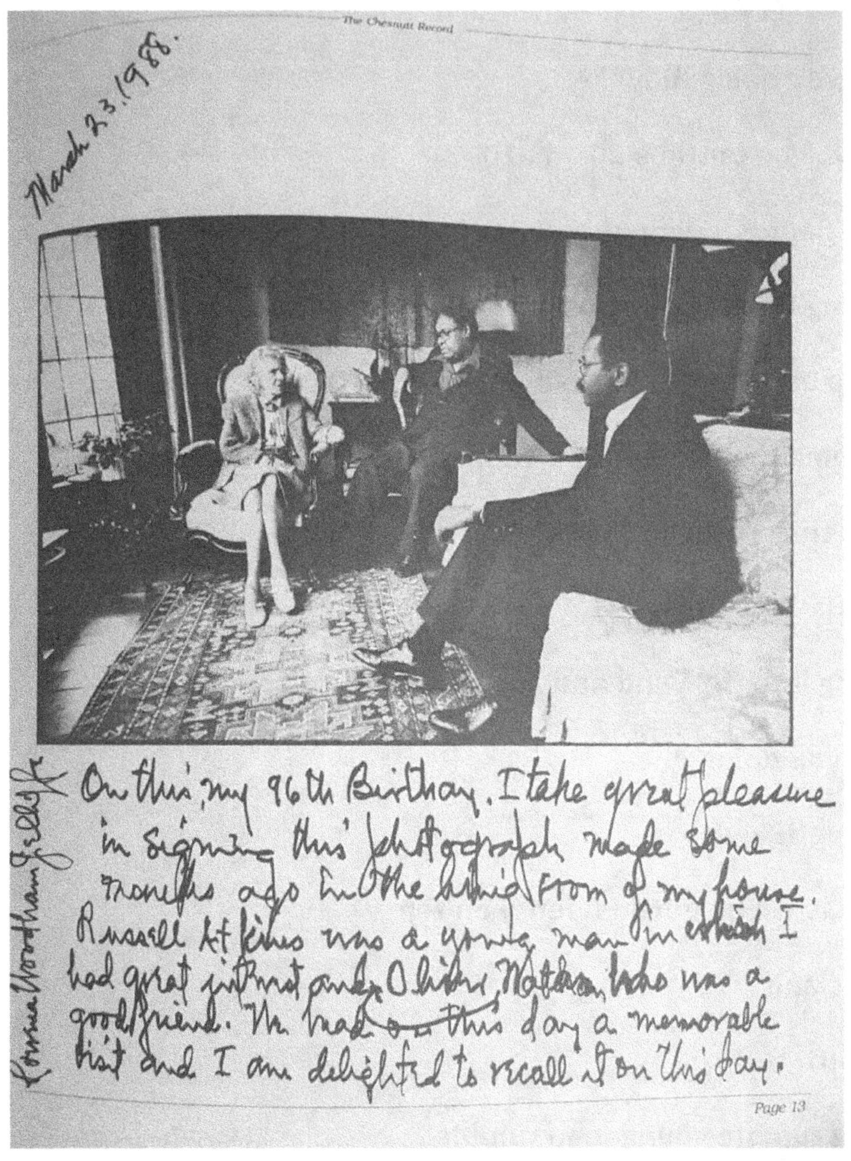

Part of the feature article on Russell Atkins in the *Chesnutt Record*

Pouring Water on a Drowning Man

Standing in a blizzard.

 Splitting rain drops with a hammer

Crossing over into a place that erases broken promises of failure

Walking through rivers of sorrow

Watching the meaning of love vanish,

With the smell of consequences.

   Slowly skipping along the edges of tomorrow,

Watching the misery of some long tyme since been gone.

Waiting for an answer from before, maybe after.

I see the glitter in your eyes, smell the sorrow of luster lost escaping

From your soul.

   Millie tells a story about a NICKEL AND A NAIL.

Ludella catches the Katie.

Empty places, lonely faces, forgotten spaces, broken hearts.

Standing in a dark alley being shadowed by death and Chaney.

   Muddy Waters whispers another mule is kicking in his stall.

Along came B,B, KING ,Freddie King ,Albert KING ,Willie King,ZZ Hill.

Telling about the Sun House and the T-Bone.

Somewhere near someplace close to someone stands a man whispering

A prayer to a lost soul.

The Muntu Poets

Full of empty meanings and broken promises waiting for a tomorrow to come save

The day that never was.

Original Muntu Poets (left to right): Yahya Sabur, Mutawaf Shaheed,
and Yaseen Assami
(Photo credit: K Kelly McElroy)

RAC--IT!!!

Moving closer to the tyme when Willie-B will come ?
　BLAM !
KA-CHING
　　WHAM
　　　　BOOM
　　SCHWICH

　　　　　　　　　　o　　RING! RING!

　　CLANG!!!
Suddenly the door slams and the window breaks.,
　　BOOM ! !.
　　　CRACKLE

　　　PING
I Hear someone singing in the background.
　　who is it?
　　　　WHO IS IT ?
　　　　　WHO THE HELL? IS IT ?
CLANG
　CLANG
　　　CLANG
　POO-NANNY ! !
　　　　　STOP THAT RAC-IT,
one long one short two tweets and a whistle and a tear
　　　somewhere between now and then
　　　close to never lost between commitment and self
　distruct.
　　　stands the empty vessel that father called a heart
　　　　further on down the road you will accompany me
　　　in a space and tyme close to a lost luve and a scream

i stand whispering into a place where life has no meaning or purpose'

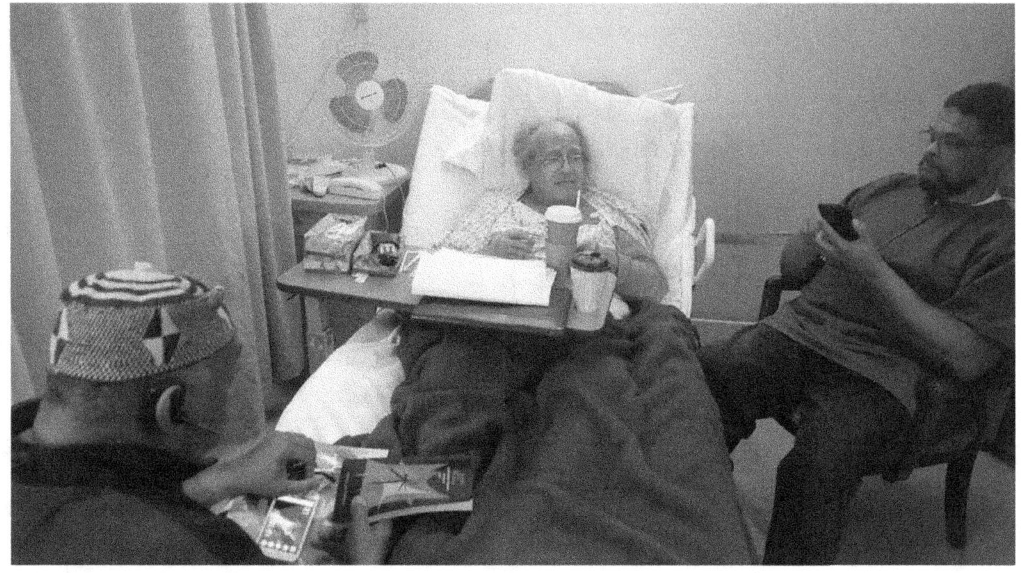

Original Muntu Poets Yaseen Assami (far left) and Mutawaf Shaheed (far right) visiting Russell Atkins (center)
(Photo credit: K Kelly McElroy)

Original Muntu Poets Elmer Buford and Mutawaf Shaheed
(Photo credit: K Kelly McElroy)

Elmer Buford

Basic Composition

Completeness:/
 Begins not at/
  birth,/
   which is life
But the relationship/
  in particular, particular
Again to whatever/
  range of experiences
The whole/
  which may or/
   may not share:
But begins through/
  process of cogent
Changes/
  which yields,/
   to a basic/
    composition, me

04/26/1968

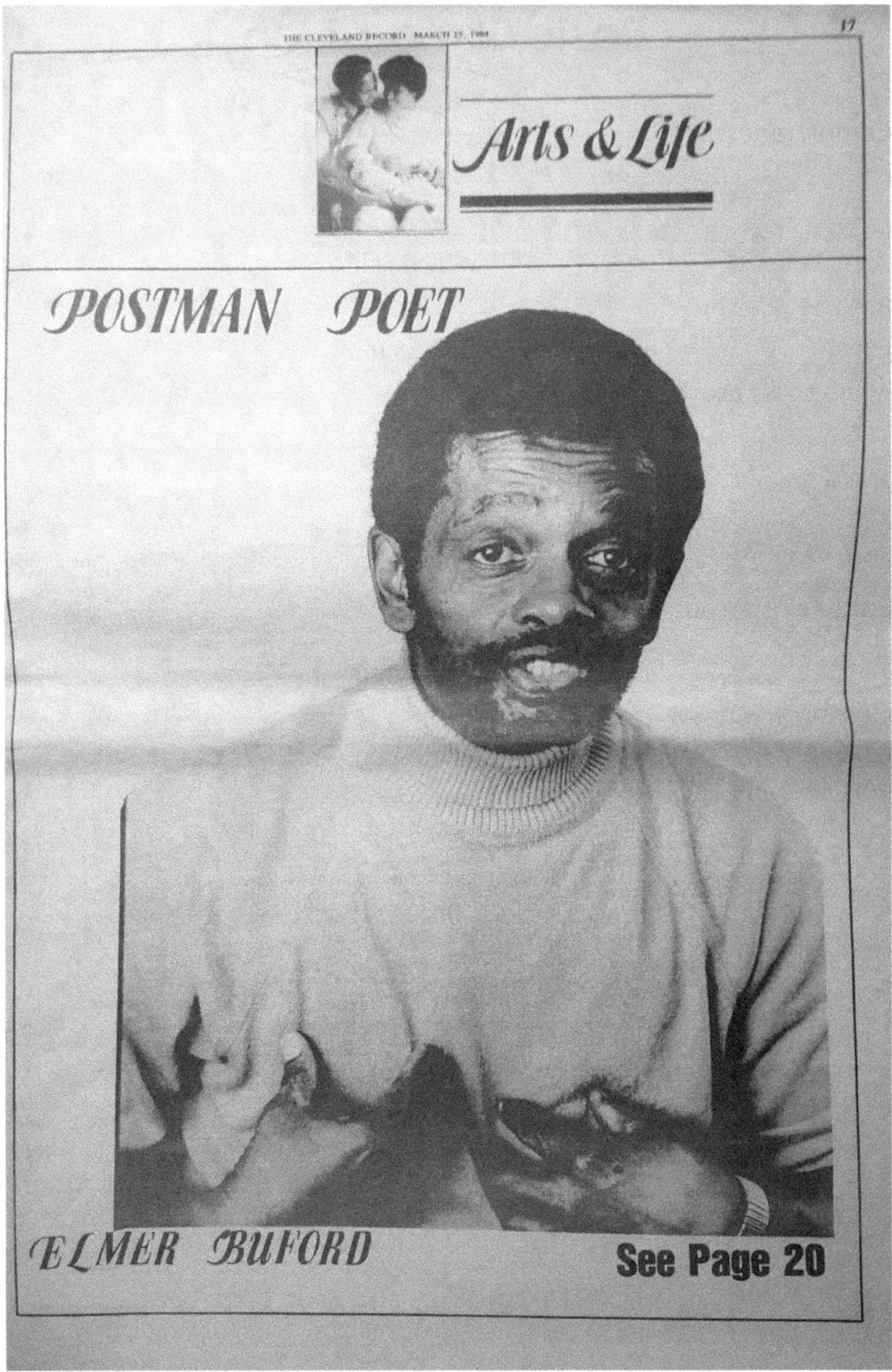
THE CLEVELAND RECORD   MARCH 15, 1984

17

Arts & Life

POSTMAN POET

ELMER BUFORD

See Page 20

Diseased Beans

The daughters of/
          Solomon toil in
Bean fields of/
          Kentucky bending theirs
Backs low to/
          The earth, stripping
Each vibe of/
          Its pods and/
               Heritage
And the master/
          Astride his great
White stallion rides/
          Slowly between long
Aisles of endless/
          Labor throwing beans
At the buttocks/
          Of future mistresses

               05/18/1968

The postman poet

I'm Black

I look at my skin...it is black
I look at my hair...it is kinky
I look at my hands...are they not part of the human man?
I look at my feet...each has five toes, not webbed.
I look at my nose, a little flat, but it is not long like an elephant's snout.
I look at my legs...perhaps not the most beautiful, but not spindly like the ostrich.
I look at my home...a ghetto in the flats.
I sleep...I eat like any other man
I laugh...I weep like all men do at sometime or the other
I think...And I worry from time to time
I even lie infrequently
I love life
I want it to be full and meaningful...
My blood is red...so is the white man's
It flows through arteries, viens and capillaries...
Is this so unique in that I am black?
I'm capable of propagating...
I ask myself and I ask you, too, white man;
Am I so foul, so degenerated that the mere mentioning of my name Colored, negro, blackie, coon or your pet cliche, "boy", brings to your senses utter contempt which eats away at your soul like cancer?
Am I so contagious that my very existence is a menace to your supposedly thoroughbred race?
What then makes me so "rare a creature" within the human race?
Silver and gold have I none
But yet I know...I have soul...soul...soul
Soul that is deep, soul that is pure
And then you, you white man stand back and aloof
Clinging to you "sanctified ideals of racial purity"
While upon your shoulders you wear the "cape of awe" and from your "tarnished silver" tongue you spew a venom more deadly than an "adder's" bite. With your most polite sarcasm...quote "Is this a negro..?
He looks like a man but so ononery, a woman beater
I hate but don't know completely why, mainly, he's black"
Yes I am black...
I shall not, I will not retract
I shall not get back
I shall, I will be heard like a voice crying in the wilderness.
I'm black, a black beauty that shines brighter than all the asteroids and Galaxies that heaven can assemble
For I'm black, black, black...

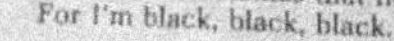

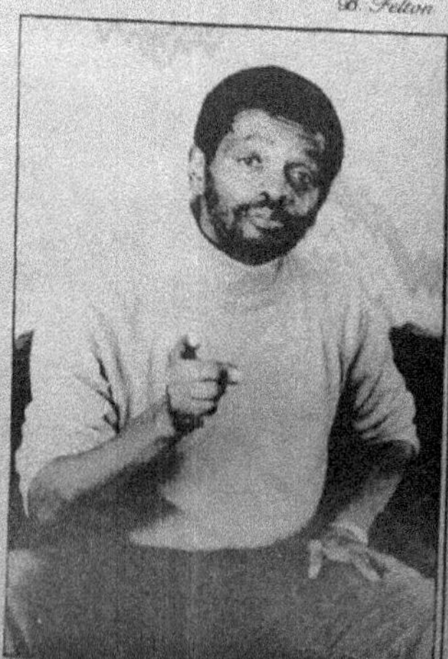

Feeling Vibrations

I feel vibrations,/
              trickling pulsations/
                          of life
Moving throughout this/
              maze of protoplasm
With blinding speed/
              in sequence, orbiting
The mind with/
             criminal intent,/
                    strumming upon the
Senses wildly:/
             like a guitar/
                  badly out of/
                        tune
As laughing voices/
             gather buttercups:/
                    Small
Children wading through/
              a stream splashing
Tiny feet in/
          soft silt beneath/
              a glassy surface.
Slip off blue-jeans,/
             Sneakers/
                Slide beneath the
Liquid dome/
          move nimbly about/
                like fish

                    12/15/1967

Love's Dimensions

Love that can be gentle, has many dimensions....

But only when such dimensions are parallel and symbolic....

Comprehensive, that the intricate pattern it forms cannot be

Duplicated, or likely fabricated by the wayward symbols

Or illusions of life....

Published 1971, authored by B Felton (aka Elmer Buford), forward by
Russell Atkins

The Thief

With curled talons night came...
To steal summer from the air
Little breath, sweet and fair
Snatched in its prime.
Night did dare...
Summer was there, chilled, pale.
The sprite now gone...
Summer faced the dawn.
Night had won, stolen the play...
Summer was gone...

05/26/1961

Robert Fleming

a group of Negro writers

the wise ones parrot the words they learn

mulatto minded and mighty egos

love to lounge in rattan chairs

wily native waiters at the fingertips

tinted glasses covering their bloodshot eyes

a throbbing circle of intellect

protected by a solid glass barrier

of newsprint politics and prejudiced pens

occasionally one would rise

and press his face and hands smack

against the invisible strength

features flat kiss the eyes see squish

helpless because they want

to be heard outside of the neighborhood

these quivering brains drained by the media

a collection of shock sighted ranting chic children

shaking their small fists

at their heroes on television.

BLACK WOMEN (from an admirer)

Flowers beyond category

they who put lighting over our heads

they who put lightning in our wills

and blow and blow and blow

yourself out   she screamed

shrill   shriek knives with their invisible hands

cut slice thin deep lines into the flesh of the soul

her pain our pain   her blues our blues

always down low

like a broken radio with a lazy speaker

she the other part of the unknown

bleeds alone in a shadow room

the crazed cats inside her   whirling

in mid-air tangled

and blow and blow and blow

yourself out   she screamed

only she sees her self

slide to the floor   moaning

for the wild pieces that never come home

so she cries

over the toilet so he'll never know

her pain our pain

even when she stands   by the mike

walking around on her hands

hoping to lure us to her face

we see the wrong way.

H E R O D

To listen them talk   I am

The monster   The slayer of newborns

The biblical murderer with the cold convict

face and frog voice   Why I never let

strangers sit too long in my house

or memories linger   Or the reason

for my orphan life

I never killed Christ   If they would

just listen listen and forget the name

that I am.

THE WISDOM
OF THE ELDERS

J U J U

This swirling power inside me

Speaks when there is nothing inside but sores

Void of the healing spirit as the word LOVE

Ever see the glow of the black cat's eyes at night

It is me without pins and dolls

Someone's revenge upon you

Without leaving a trace someone's wounded.

Juju for shadow people trapped in a steel world

Even the fresh blood like me knows

As I move closer to truth

To the other side of my breath

To the earth history of my color awaiting me in the distance.

Yet I hold my course due South like my ancestors

Toward the drum talk   toward the cane and cotton fields

But the veterans say

That we laborers can never own our own souls.

GIFT
OF TRUTH
ROBERT FLEMING

Poem for Beginners

deep in the outburst of their misery

the fat gobbling cream puffs to hide their tears

steeped in colors of charcoal

with backstage tales of porcelain

children raising cain

mammies penned to the mat

underneath layers of makeup and clothes

designed for the perfect rape victim

and sit and sit and sit still

with daytime peace work nightmares

charming they feets

and flattening they battle scarred nights

say to say to never step on anybody's toes

and to keep your behind stuck up in the back

like a black ant

deep in the outburst of their misery

the poor are always in error

their ghosts always out of bounds

as the poor await their debut

while their heads are still warm

dealing with an array of friends from the Big House

for a sniff of slop and a scholarship to charm school

savage this life

episodes of routine trips to the cleaners

from a catalogue of split decisions

hocus-pocus for the Pure-D depraved

yo-yos for the kiddies trapped in bodies burning up

strange as it seems

fido was born old to learn the necessary tricks

his tambourine tuned up too high

so sick believing that we're living at their expense

so sick believing that slaves can be freed with a song

our folks are in love with dinner music

filled with glee for a pat on the head

for good luck

sorry our beginners have no trumps

milk the coma from our mirage

bring a halt to this eternal honeymoon

accomplished in the backseat joy of our delusions

with no place to call our own

with no title to anything

but our obsession

for bloomers and thrills

hey junebug...some like it hot!

ROBERT FLEMING
Author of After Blood
When you cross the line
there's no turning back...
Fever In The Blood

Pyramid (in tribute to firearms)

Niggers with fuses blown

most of us forgot to order replacements

and our argyles

bring us to know roscoe.

He spits bullets. Much silver at night.

Up on the peak of panting and thrusting

the moment of knee burns and callouses

the dark hand caressing fur

and closing upon its metal hardness.

For guns are sexual to some.

Art Nixon

Highway Markers, Review Mirrors –
For Cheryl

Inside the car
In the mirror
The sky has just dissolved a red tablet of sun
And dyed itself   hot pink   maroon
And   now,   black.

Mute and rejected & filed at less than mile intervals
The highway markers sprout in the headlight spray
And wither red in the taillights passing.
The Truth Is:
In the beginning was the end.
Even
The
Orgasm

Begins in a thin wheeze of need,
But soon becomes
A glorious megaphone
Announcing its own
Departure

Even
The
Mystics have sometimes taught there is a death
After life after death...

The shoe presses down and the markers rush up
To the windows like obedient phantoms
Where you see them for what they are:
Cheap fixtures to be jettisoned from

The Muntu Poets

The night-long room,
Flash passed and gulped up by the blackness
Leaning full-blown and immovable
All across the car's rear view:
Each beginning existing at the mercy of an ending.

It is what it means
To see chunks
Of highway night-space
After each marker that is passed.
It is what someone said
They thought you should have been;
And *more* than you knew yourself to be
It is what it means to have been legally in love.

The highway markers will parade infinity
Across one more state line

Before the night begins to nod,,
It's last cup of strong black coffee
loosened from its fingers

And spills onto the asphalt in an

Obscene libation:

Finally, the night,

Supine in the middle of

The highway: shoeless,

Dirty sock soles on one foot,

The other barefoot,

Will lay with its mouth gaped bright blue.

From time   to   time   it is
The rearview that is viewed and reviewed
That   mirrors   the   wall of black
You've been speeding through,
With not a trace to betray your direction.
 From   time   to   time until
The Light: the eyes will check.

They *know* there can be
New beginnings   but seem   to   need   more proof,
That you've been
Where you've been

--Art Nixon/1977

Russell Atkins reviews two books published by Uptown Publishing
(Photo credit: Mutawaf Shaheed)

[In Confidence]

Sometimes I awake
In the middle of the night
and I am not there

I have slipped away:
Like a well-used bar of soap in the shower, or
The first dime through a new hole in a worn pocket,
The shadow of a good point--meant to be made--in the heat of
debate, or
That fat, yellow balloon-moon tethered to the car for miles, then
look again
And it is trapped in a tree, blocked by a billboard, or replaced by a
mountain.

I lie there
Fascinated yet overwhelmed
At the terror of being outside myself:
My name and all genetics
Bled out into blackness, deafening silence, immovable and eternal

I brace against its unmentionable depth, and
Sense the length of the unfathomable
that I am in this place

I inhabit your weight next to me,
Listen to the sleeping softness of your breaths
And wonder what it's made of:

Curiously I touch the dark/gather it
In my fingers and brush up against the
Awful weight of miracles compressed into
This moment,

This unexpected Presence
This witnessing of God
So polite
So quiet
So discrete...
Merely shifting positions
In the room
When He
Thought
I was
Asleep
--Art Nixon 2001

Art Nixon is a contributing writer in the *Voices from Leimert Park: a poetry anthology*

La Curandera on Monterey Road -
for Maria

You

magic lady, even before I knew your name

Pushed buttons you had no right to have in your possession.

You,

Hibiscus-scented sorceress, carried with you

in the secret pockets

Of your black Donna Karan, ground length poncho,

The maps to places in my heart I swore never, ever existed.

You,

With your Rainforest hair of moonless nights

And lips the color of heart-blood

Till this day pierce me with dried Arizona cactus thorns & thistles where

It hurts...yet feels too good to breathe,

That place where you press the thumb against the heart.

2.

In a trance

The Muntu Poets

I have followed you into the desert at night,

Like a child promised endless sweets the color of gemstones.

There,

On the moon-washed desert floor

Your eyes command me to sit,

To watch you disrobe & move

Naked

And wild

And raunchy to sounds that only you can hear:

      the stomping of sharp-booted heels

       on hard flamenco wood,

       stomping faster & faster in a

Mad race of staccato clapping and racing fingers

Over guitar strings greased with fresh habanero,

Faster and faster that only your head can hear.

Your body,

The texture of damp moss at dawn—spinning

Your body

Musking the place between sand & diamond-blasted night sky

With the heavy ripe of fresh slit cantaloupe and salty Gamay—
Twirling &

Gyrating & undulating—shaking stars loose with your hips and finger
tips,

Squatting & Arching

—*Lo quiero ahora!!*

Stomping & pumping

—*Lo quiero ahora!*

Pumping and pitching

—*Lo quiero ahora!*

Pulsing & promising

Gone &...

...Vanished.

In my head

Your voice echoes your home-grown

Riddle of senseless charm but deadly spell—

The Muntu Poets

The only incantation you know:

> *Lust is love and love is lust,*

> *Make one your hearts desire*

> *But never ever trust trust*

i sit bewitched,

 touched crazy mad in a moon-soaked desert,

The breeze disguised as your breath on my neck,

Your laughing wrapped in wind...

3.)

In my bed. Alone.

I rationalize you into something I can handle: Like

Burning up bad karma.

Mid-life confusion.

An inconvenient period of insanity.

Or just plain old poor judgment.

But inside it is my heart

That knows I am lying.

It giggles secretly to itself,

Knowing it has been healed,

And it knows what I may never admit:

> that your spirit is pure heat,
>
> pure ice blue flame for
>
> sterilizing and cauterizing,
>
> old dreams, old wounds...
>
> and the evidence
>
> of charred moth wings
>
> will always
>
> betray
>
> your presence
>
> in the silence
>
> of my

nights.

Art Nixon/Copyright 1997

Norman Jordan. A play featuring Norman Jordan's poems debuts in London, Spring 2016

O.G. - for Alexis N.

Eternal Ace-Boons

arms linked arm-in arm

in lock-step

since time without beginning--

even before this planet had a spot

to spin on

we exchanged these Bodhisattva rings,

we shared and we share

this Buddha thing:

Sho-i-sho Nyo ze so

Nyo ze sho   Nyo ze Tai

Nyo ze riki   Nyo ze sa

Nyo ze in   Nyo ze en

Nyo ze ka   Nyo ze ho

Nyo ze honmak^kukyo---My G!!!

Some lifetimes she's been my *Sensei*

and I her assigned hand servant,

she's been my mama,

my daughter

my husband

She's been my dog and me hers,

my muse, my distraction, my disciple

We've been bitter cellmates sentenced to

the same hermaphroditic shell

in at least a couple of lifetimes,

arguing, bickering, try'n to catch

Musta been something I did this last time

'cause it took me half this lifetime

to catch up with you this time

in this city of angels and demons

Didn't fool me. I read the clues:

same initials we share. Same North Side, Pittsburgh birthplace.

read the Lotus sutra in your eyes. Straight-up *Knew* who you was

despite your having gone behind my back,

cashed-in a fist-full of *my* karmic bonus points

and showed up in *this* lifetime

as out-of-control gorgeous with nutmeg for freckles

and that beast-taming grin:

Yeah, that's right--straight up recognized ya!

Talk'n shit. Exhaling Virginia Slims out the corner of your mouth,

slipping compassion like bidness cards

to grimy souls on the QT,

trolling and strolling

that furry pet you secretly

told me you called "Big Mystic" on

a short leash & wearing your trademark

silk boxers--**MY *G!!***

My *G!!*

My Ms black Dickies work pants wearing

The Muntu Poets

Dap-Daddy. Double butch-down. Dudette.

Strapped in with suspenders and no nonsense shoes,

Porkpie broke way down

over the eyes--not for affect--but as a private partition

for strong & direct eye contact

before she gets all up in my head

all up in my head,

she's a Buddha Gangster

in a slit evening gown and slut-pumps: *working it!*

her gown riding upper thigh high and not in the least self-conscious;

with pumps kicked off for more grip: *gone work this!*

Gone git to the bottom of this,

Gone thug some enlightenment up out

The steel compartments of my self-delusions and

Half-ass perpetrations, Gone make Ugly Truths

Rise...Rise...RISE...big-bitch-on-up outta there...

And waddle casually across the floor where I'm living.

We share the laughter of punch lines

to jokes we made up thousands of years ago

We move in and out

and around and thru each other's spirit

as though they were second homes

And sleep deeply and well

because we found out: *Again,*

In this lifetime,

Who's got

Our

Back

-Art Nixon 2006

Art Nixon is a contributing writer in *Catch the Fire!!! A Cross-Generational Anthology of Contemporary African-American Poetry*

Smooth Science

There was a time
When I would
Coax the light back out of the dawn
With my tongue

And gloat over
The infinite
Elixirs I'd brew
With my words

A time when I would stand my ground
Inside my young black skin &
Beg for leg
Like a country boy in bib overalls,
With the Harvest Moon in my voice
And pockets full of
Smooth large stones

So pregnant with myself
I would take a woman's first rejections
As a down payment for my services to be rendered,
A command to lean forward in my science
Explode out the blocks & skim low & quick
Whisking dimes off the tops of hurdles with my ass...

Moons wane.
Petulant waves race after its own impulse/
Eventually receding to low tide/gathered up in the arms of the sea

    Retreating like a woman's desire,
    Kidnapped by her own intuition

Stout trees prop up the skies

The Muntu Poets

And the oak is eventually felled,
It's accountability of time
Irrefutable--right there--in the simple arithmetic
Of its own cross sections

I have traveled the long way around the mountain
To respect the forces that dwell
In the spaces between my words

These days
If I tell you that you are beautiful
You need not take it personally:

I am just the weatherman, baby
Smiling kindly inside the TV box,
Pointing my wand at the map,
And wouldn't dare take the credit
For a sunny day

--Art Nixon/3-31-01

CLEVELAND ETHICAL SOCIETY

Member of the American Ethical Union

3602 MENLO ROAD • CLEVELAND, OHIO 44120

A fellowship without creed or dogma, dedicated to the cultivation of ethical values in human relations, affirming that the highest spiritual values are to be found in man's relation to man......

PROGRAM FOR SUNDAY – MAY 5, 1968
Music School Settlement 11125 Magnolia Dr.

Introductory Music: Coltrane

Introduction of the Program: Mrs. Bernard Pucker

THE MUNTU WORKSHOP OF CLEVELAND

(Black Creative Writers Workshop)

Featuring

Mr. Norman Jordan   Mr. Clyde Shy

Mr. Bill Russell   Mr. Amir Rashidd

The social hour which follows the meeting is intended to give us an opportunity for fellowhip along with our tea and coffee. We cordially invite you to join us.

Social hour hosts today are: Mr. & Mrs. George Goldsmith

Future Programs

May 12   "Four Professors Look at the University: Economics, Politics, and Philosophy." Panel participants; Dr. Samuel Gorovitz, Dept. of Philosophy, Dr. David Miller, Dept. of Religion, Dr. Terrance Mitchell, Metallurty Div. of the School of Engineering, Dr. Kenneth Wiskind, Fluid Sciences Div. the School of Engineering, all of Case Western Reserve University.

May 19   Miss Geraldine Williams, now a candidate for Congress in the 21st district.

Coming Events

There will be baked goods for sale immediately after todays program.

May 19   Membership Meeting – here – 8:00p.m. A reception for new members will follow.

Amir Rashidd

A BLUE FUNK PIECE – for Freddie King/ a Boogie Man

Heat treated salt blood
blue green sweat
and those days whip lashed
and coin phrased

A blind man
A rough shuffle stamp
like sand bag thighs
like Bodosha women
Sunday humming and down
beating for
high strung loves
Like buck dance children
eating flesh dirt
and raw peanuts

It is like the softest voice
against the hardest refrain and
it is as sensuous as
new south winds
trading toe tappings
with stone clouds
trotting the lightening
skies of this love
pure ebony as all silence

sweet blood call

The Poetry of
Amir Rashidd

Illustrated by
Lois Griffith

FOR THE ANTHROPOLOGICAL VISITORS

The night breath hung frigid
and the fossiled years wound by
on three legged horses
and raving men

Streaks of winding kight came
in with the echoes and disputed laughter
Reasons folded like broken nipples
like eyes upon the reaching sky

It is all colorless
and you came one sided
into this cultural spectrum
You came inside volting pules
and sophisticated rhetoric
empty eyes sweeping and rattling
mouths foaming against
rust iron graves and
crumbled village fences

Your blasted faces searching
gazing into thevanished years
Gawking into an undiscovered past
and realizing nothing

Russell Atkins reviews the *Our Young Voices* flagship publication
(Photo credit: Mutawaf Shaheed 2015)

IN SEARCH FOR A POEM

Far away dreams
remote flowers and
primitive spirits of
indigo tongues

Over the purple whisk
the night fled
like startled children
hungry in the wilds

the overlook sky
is suddenly
apprehended by
a stark beauty

Where in a caravans deep
inside my
silent self
travel uncertain
shadows

Seeking
merely nomad
destinations

Norman Jordan was an internationally known poet who made his home in Fayette County, West Virginia. Jordan, pictured here in the African American Heritage Family Tree Museum which he founded in Ansted, West Virginia, was also well-known for his portrayal of figures such as Carter G. Woodson and as a playwright and arts administrator.

PICK'N COTTON - for Ottis Spann -

I am song of
ANCESTOR
       / of the flesh and
              Bone

In that part of your
skull

ANCESTOR

from where i
came

coming with
part of
your face

ANCESTOR

and all of
your magic song

i am song of

ANCESTOR
       / of the flesh and
              Bone

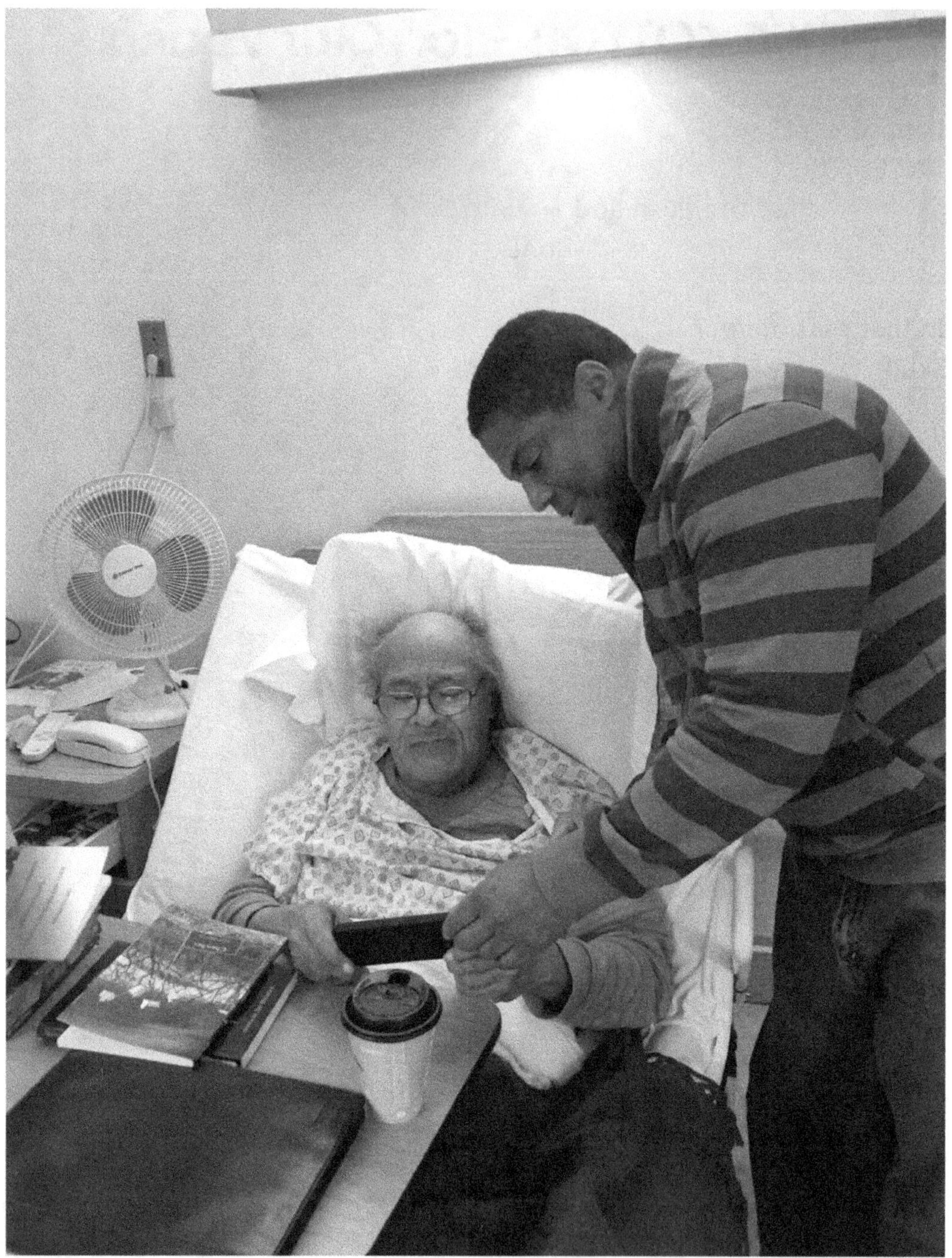

Russell Atkins with Publisher/Filmmaker K Kelly McElroy
(Photo credit: Mutawaf Shaheed)

The Beast - for Fred Ahmed Evans 02/10/1967 A.D. -

Beneath the tall and shadowy trees
My brother black danced with ease
And yet the morning brought disaster
The beast is coming faster, faster.

My brothers black withheld their pride
They went so far as suicide
They surely knew that death held no pains
The beast is coming with shackling chains.

He burned my farm and slashed my arm
And brought me far from home
Across the sea to the land of the free
The beast is coming to burn your home.

The beast said we were ignorant
Said we were totally incompetent
Yes, we won his wars and grew his crops
The beast is coming, your freedom to stop.

Brothers black please hear the cry
Our mothers weep, our fathers sigh
Black men brothers black we're free
Let's fight and die for land you see.

War with the beast, it must be won
The task of fate has now begun
We must strike with such great pain

So that the beast will never rise again.
Brothers black all free men cry
We've won our life through endless plights
Brothers black walk without sigh
The beast is dead, hear freedom cry.

CLEVELAND ETHICAL SOCIETY

Member of the American Ethical Union

3602 MENLO ROAD • CLEVELAND, OHIO 44120

THE MUNTU WORKSHOP OF CLEVELAND

AMIR RASHIDD is a charter member of the Muntu Workshop.
He has given many readings. He has read his work at Duke University,
Pitt University and others. He was a guest reader at the anti-Vietnam
peace rally in Washington and has been mentioned in several publications
including the Negro Digest. His booklet of poetry, "The End of Truth's
Beginning", has just been issued.

BILL RUSSELL has been an editor of Voice, the house organ for
a government program. His poems have appeared in several places, viz.,
Vibration and Free Lance Magazine's Langston Huges issue. He will appear
in the Muntu Workshop Journal and is scheduled for readings at several
colleges. He does wood sculpturing also.

CLYDE SHY is a musician as well as a poet. He has traveled
in Europe with the Charles Tyler Trio and has a profound interest in
astrology. His appearances include recitals of poetry with music at
Core's Target City Festival during Black Arts week and at Diogenes'
Lantern under Community Colleges auspices and at the Institute of Gestalt
Therapy. His poems are scheduled for the Muntu Workshop Journal and
reprints from Right Angle, a company newspaper.

NORMAN JORDAN is the Director of the Black Creative Writers
Workshop or "Muntu" Workshop of Cleveland, members of which are those
whose names are listed above. Mr. Jordan's plays have been performed
by the San Diego State College drama Department. His poems have been
accepted by Soulbook, SNCC's Afro-American Magazine and Black Poets Journal.
He is schedlued to appear in the anthology edited by Lawrence Neal and
LeRoi Jones and in the new edition of The Huges-Bontemps anthology.

Yahya A. Sabur (Jon Hall)

Change

Mind was not made to dwell
on one thought
but to explore and find out
  what life is about
People in a rut soon find themselves
enslaved, chained not by iron
    just day to day----Struggle
to free your mind
 go and seek fulfillment
find out the beauty that living can bring
  understand your fellow man
grasp a thought and follow your star..

When i finally realized that
Man's struggle would not always
preoccupy me, when i recognized
that there would come the day
when something else would inspire me;
i became confused and dumbfounded
at this aspect of life, but i lay
wait for this grand day-
For the shelf that i'm on leads towards
decay
i would like to speak of that change
i see, a greater meaning for being here,
of love for the Highest Being

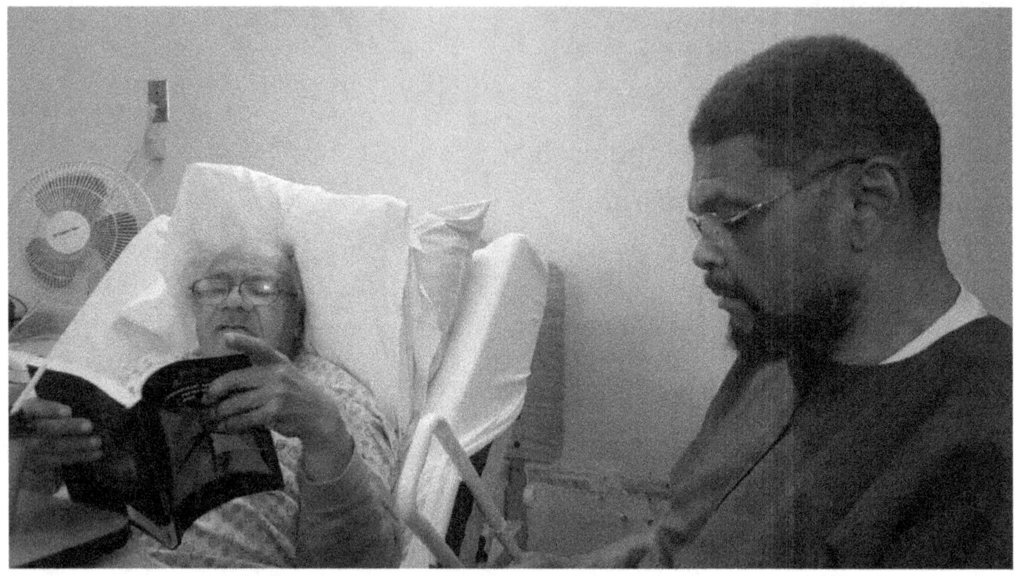

Russell Atkins with Original Muntu Poet Mutawaf Shaheed
(Photo credit: K Kelly McElroy)

Clear Evidence

in the name of Allaah, Most Gracious, Most Merciful   clear
evidence

it is a matter of faith
that brings about the
fact of the matter...
faith put into practice
which brings about change

methods of conduct which eradicate
barriers of ignorance
resulting in states
of concern, manners of
redress--hope based
on clear evidence
clear evidence
of the morning light
which follows the
darkness of deprivation
the clear evidence illustrated
by the flowers
that bloom in fields that
were once bare of herbage

Original Muntu Poets (left to right): Yahya Sabur, Mutawaf Shaheed, and Yaseen Assami
(Photo credit: K Kelly McElroy)

Dark Shadows

dark shadows
move into confronted
camps
instant dismay
to the chosen few
what is the
wind that produces
such?
what is the meaning
of this omen?
in structure,
this substance
seems the
same
unproportionate
disagreement on
its name---
seeds lie
wasted on
unproductive soil
no one toils
the earth---
barren thorns
catch minds
and leave them as
evidence of
chaotic times

Yahya Sabur is a contributing writer in the *New Black Poetry* anthology

Half-Empty

half-empty, half-full

  too little, too late,
words
misused, contorted,
bent out of shape---

hate-monger, fire bomber,
  thug, thief,
ascribed to those
  who prophesize
fate
  be cool, don't wait,
get it together---it's too late

  listen to the meaning,
not only the sound,
  get with the feeling,
mode and time
let it not run like water
thru a sieve-like
  mind
  let your words
be bullets, and
  your mind the
gun

and blast! when you
observe

 the whites of
their eyes.

Russell Atkins. (Photo credit Charles Pinkney, charlespinkney.com)

Limited Dreams

in the name of Allah, Most Gracious, Most Merciful

limited dreams

ever had a dream that is so strange, so bizarre that your only thoughts
are to escape ...causing to wake up only then you drift back to sleep
only to find yourself in the same dream making what some call
progress
but you finally realize as marching in place like running a threadmill
like a mouse, running thru a maze, winding up right where you started
..
the subject of the mad scientist's experiment
generating energy for someone else's benefit
what others might preceive as a dream, i conclude
is the reality of live in america

successful minimalist starting off
as inspired rebels find themselves
coopted as spokemen for
the trappings of success
which in reality are the
chains of capital slavery, capital lynching
which cannot be broken
by any means necessary

we must wake up to the
truth that the Most Praiseworthy, who has
given us the bounty of intellect enabling

us to determine light from darkness,
sweet from bitter, soothing melodies
from harsh sounds
pleasant aromas from odious pollution
has also given us messages and messengers
that provide us examples of living right(the truth)
as opposed to doing wrong and
being misled to believe we are
having "a good time"

Norman Jordan was a member of the Griot Collective Poetry Workshop of Jackson, Tennessee. In 2008, he became an official member of the Affrilachian Poets of Lexington, Kentucky.

Mutawaf A. Shaheed (C. E. Shy)

Advancing

Things never changed much for the Dumb Cluck.
Oh, he still had a cold one in the fridge, the TV still
worked. His boss, who he never met wasn't
going to give him a lower mortgage or the 401k back.
He didn't drop the cost of the beer or cigarettes.
No matter how much he did for his boss his situation
was not going to ever change. The stories he loved,
that kept him entertained they wouldn't change either.
He was so dumb that he thought he was doing good for
his folks. The mirrors in his house didn't work either so
he just removed them , like Dracula. Blood is what he
had in common with the count. His boss actually hated
 him and would thank whoever he believed in for the Cluck.
All the time his boss was trying to get away and leave the
Cluck where he found him, because he was not going to take
him with them for sure! When the Cluck got home from a
night of pure hatred he still had cancer, His wife was still
cheating on him, his kids were using heroin.
The doctor bills kept skyrocketing for the 3 dogs. His
neighbor was found to be a serial killer. The guy across
 the street was a school teacher and a pedophile.
He was so screwed up his answer to everything was to
 murder, torture
everybody. He still didn't get a raise. Nothing changed.
Some how he was advancing the cause of humanity.
Well, that's what the TV told him.

Time Share
C.E. Shy

Tabulations

The regrets were lodged in groups.
 They were in numbers that were
random. They were arranged from the
things he could remember clearly
and the ones he wanted to forget.

 There were the ones that his numbed
conscience would not let him find. The
ones drenched in blood he could
rationalize those. He would compare
them to mosquitoes.

He never regretted his idea that water
was not a right but a privilege. Killing the
poor was his answer to poverty. He was
Pissed off because he couldn't find any one
else in the universe to murder.

At his job he was given a corner office, which
 he destroyed within a weeks time. He wanted
to kill his boss because he fired him. He regretted
the fact he couldn't find him. He couldn't imagine
why he got fired! It just didn't add up.

Substitutions
C.E. Shy

The Asterisk

I'm a butcher*, a chef* .I make
candy and candles*

I'm a cop*. I'm a fireman*
I'm a teacher*, a scientist*

I'm an athlete*, a programmer*
a photographer*, a kid*

I'm a reporter*, a cameraman*,
 a criminal*, a clown*. I'm a businessman*

I'm a doctor*, a lawyer*, an Indian chief*
I sell insurance* and cars and trucks*

I'm a soldier* a chemist* **a clergy** * a priest*
I'm a linguist*a genius*.I'm a writer*, a poet*

I 'm etcetera*and etcetera* and etcetera*

I'm an American asterisk* Ask them.

ECLECTIONS 2

The Corporation

Pickled people spend mind money
and Nano hours twisting the truth

Making lies fit between the lines.
When they grew up they threw up from the

stuff they couldn't swallow. Designed
minds follow tips from tricksters. They

sit on a hill wiping their behind with bills
they can't spend. Damn even the honey

in the ham is fake! Potty trained puppets
piss on Que.-----Let me pause a minute

and take another drink!------. They told
me that my nightmares were just dreams

That their plans weren't really schemes.
It was 11pm when I saw the late night

blues. Trifling and trembling he stood
before the mike. The whole world listened

Then he said, " Psych!".

Eclections 3

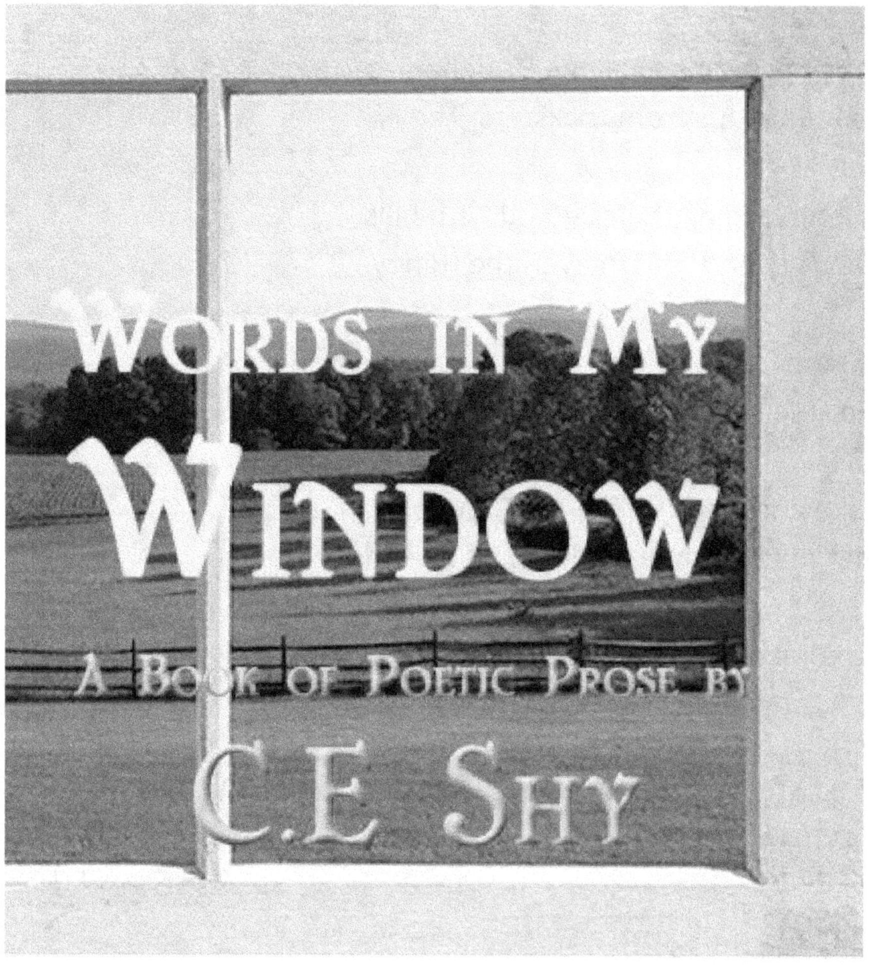

Un Natural Organs

I don't blame the butterfly for fleeing.
The bumblebee was just being.
Buzzing and croaking frogs choking
running from the flakes
of snow.

No news from Honeysuckle Rose after we
found metal on her petals. Inside plants
hide from the rain. Outside they grow in painful
circumstances.

C. E.
ROUSTING
ROBY
FROM
SHY

About the Muntu Poets

The Muntu Poets - a forgotten voice in the mid to late 60's in the city of Cleveland - was an entity that was a product of its time. There were no membership cards or applications to fill out or any barrier to be a Muntu Poet. It was a fluid entity that existed for people in the area waiting to be exposed to poetry and to the technicalities of writing poetry.

For the most part, the majority of the poets were young, movement conscious, energetic and upset with the status quo. There wasn't anyone who was laboring under any illusions about our plight. Everyone expressed themselves in different ways I'd say. The poets read all over the place, including in other states, for the better part of 67/68 under the banner of Muntu.

The workshop took place once a week at a place on Superior Avenue and Ansel Road on the second floor of the building. There were folks present who were poets before the workshop and people who were there just to check out what was going on.

There was an eclectic group of styles present. The voices of dissent were the loudest and it was this group that raised their voices everywhere they went. In their view, there was nothing pretty or funny about the circumstances Black people were in. They were the only group of poets in the city doing that. They felt that everyone else was putting honey and perfume on shit. The poets who had a similar outlook were the ones who usually read together at various venues around the country.

The last time that the group officially met was on July 23rd of 1968 at 10518 Elk Avenue. That day, (the beginning of the Glenville Riots) was what the Muntu Poets predicted was coming. Most of the poets continued to write and now they have gathered to write another anthology 47 years after the first was written. This anthology is a tribute to Russell Atkins and

Norman Jordan who were the leaders of the powerful group of writers. I'm grateful to have been a part of it.

M.A. Shaheed/ C. E. Shy

Russell Atkins

Russell Atkins is a poet, composer, theorist, editor, and leading literary innovator. He was born on February 25, 1926 in Cleveland, Ohio. He began studying piano at age seven with his mother. From childhood, he exhibited talent in painting, drawing, music, and writing. By age thirteen, he had won several poetry contests. Atkins published his first poem in 1944 in his high school yearbook. With the support of prominent literary figures, Atkins published his poetry in journals and newspapers, including *Experiment* (1947–1951) and the *New York Times* (1951).

Atkins continued his studies of music, performance, and the visual arts through Cleveland College, Cleveland Music School Settlement, Cleveland Institute of Music, Karamu Theatre, and Cleveland School of Art. This musical training is a key to Atkins's poetic style since musical structures are central in his writing.

In 1950, Atkins cofounded what is probably the oldest black-owned literary magazine, *Free Lance*, a publication of avant-garde writing that contributed to the development of New American poetry. He created a style of concrete poetry in which visual presentation of words on the page predominates. He experimented stylistically with the extreme use of the apostrophe, embedding of words within words, and use of continuous words. In the mid- 1950s, he began utilizing an abstract technique he called "phenomenalism," which juxtaposed unfamiliar and familiar elements. Atkins advocated using the imagination "to exploit range, to create a body of effect, event, colors, characteristics, moods, verbal stresses pushed to a maximum." He did not try to make his work comprehensible to casual readers but strove for dense complexity of meaning.

Atkins experimented with "poems in play forms," publishing two plays in 1954, *The Abortionist* and *The Corpse*. Like his poetry, his plays radically challenged conventions of both form and content.

In its 1955–1956 issue, *Free Lance* published Atkins's influential article, "A Psychovisual Perspective for 'Musical' Composition". Using Gestalt theory of pattern formation, Atkins argues for the brain and not the ear as the focus of composition.

In 1960 Atkins published his first collection of poetry, *A Podium Presentation*. Subsequent volumes include *Phenomena* (1961), *Objects* (1963), *Objects 2* (1964), *Heretofore* (1968), *The Nail, to Be Set to Music* (1970), *Maleficium* (1971), *Here in The* (1976), and *Whichever* (1978).

Atkins is the lead contributor in two anthologies dedicated to him, *Imaginary Crimes In Real Gardens* and *The Muntu Poets 47 Years Later*.

Norman Jordan *

Norman Jordan was born in Ansted, West Virginia in 1938, but moved to Cleveland, Ohio as a youth to attend school. Unable to stay away, Jordan returned to Ansted, West Virginia in 1977, earning a bachelor's degree from West Virginia University in theater, and then later a master's degree in African American studies from Ohio State University.

Norman Jordan was a poet and a playwright, with his works anthologized in at least 42 books of poetry, making him one of the most published Appalachian poets. His poems have appeared in *The Poetry of the Negro, Black Fire, Make a Joyful Sound: Poems for Children by A.A. Poets, In Search of Color Everywhere: A Collection of A.A. Poetry*, and *Wild Sweet Notes: Fifty years of West Virginia Poetry 1950-1999*. A voice and leading force in the Black Arts Movement, Jordan's work also appeared in journals dedicated to the movement such as *Journal of Black Poetry* and *Black World*. Jordan had also written five books of poetry: *Destination: Ashes* (1967), *Above Maya* (1971), *Where Do People In Dreams Come From And Other Poems, Two Books*, and *Sing Me Different*. In 2008, Jordan was inducted into an exclusive group of poets named the Affrilachian Poets. Jordan was also a collaborator, editor, a storyteller, and had taught at West Virginia University, among other schools.

While living in Ohio, Norman Jordan became a leading force in the Cleveland Poetry Movement, working closely with the Karamu House, the oldest African American theater in the United States, which served as a spring board for many African American artists, including Langston Hughes and Ruby Dee. Cleveland became a notable point of circulation of ideas during the Black Arts Movement.

In addition, Jordan was the president and founder of the African American Arts and Heritage Academy (AAAHA), as well as the founder and director of the African American Heritage Family Tree Museum in Ansted, West Virginia. Jordan was very active in the community, especially with youth, serving as a director of a youth camp at Camp Washington-Carver for Culture and History for many years.

Sababa Akili

Sababa Akili was born in Clarksdale Mississippi, the fourth of 13 children.

As a child growing up in the rural south, Akili, at an early age expressed his interest in being a poet/writer. From about five years old onward, he entertained his older siblings and family members with various rhymes and song lyrics that he would compose as well as perform after their long, hard day of work in the cotton fields. When asked what he was going to be when he grew up he always insisted that he was going to be a writer. The family thought this was a good lofty notion but didn't really think it too practical with all this cotton that needed picking, which in their opinion would be a much better use of the child's hands.

Klan violence, economic oppression and social degradation fueled the family's forced migration from Mississippi to Cleveland Ohio shortly after the lynching of Emmett Till, which occurred less than fifty miles from where the family lived.

Life in this northern industrial city was different from living in the Mississippi Delta, and the promise of a better life became nothing more than an empty promise for all recent migrants like Akili and his family. After Till's murder and the Montgomery bus boycott, the struggle for democracy and social equality were in full swing by now. Growing up in this era of freedom rides, sit-ins and images of black people being beaten, murdered and bombed in churches would dramatically contribute to the early activism and radicalization of Akili.

The struggle for civil rights led by Dr. King in the South and Malcolm X and the struggle for human rights in the North, were the two contending approaches; however, Akili ultimately gravitated toward Malcolm and his views on human rights and self-defense.

After the 1966 Hough rebellion, Akili connected with local poet Norman Jordan, and other black writers/poets in the Muntu Poetry Workshop. Many of the young writers were also activists, who wrote and performed their poetry at various venues throughout the Cleveland area. Akili became involved in the movement directly as a poet/political activist, immdiately caught up in the whirlwind of the black liberation movement. Urban rebellions were breaking out all over the place. Black people were organizing for freedom, justice and equality, with political campaigns to elect black mayors and politicians, organizing against racist violence and police repression.

This motion brought Akili into contact with nationally known poet/playwright and political activist Amiri Baraka who called young African-Americans to Newark in 1968 to liberate Newark from a racist political administration. The organizing effort was successful but the new mayor ended up being very weak in addressing the problems of the black masses.

As an outspoken critic of the imperialist war in Vietnam, Akili followed the lead of Muhammad Ali and others, and refused induction into the US military and was incarcerated. Following his release and a stay in Cleveland, Akili relocated to Newark to work in the rapidly developing black liberation movement.

From 1969 to 1985, the national movement takes center stage in his life. He serves as an organizer and staff to many of the various national organizing efforts such as the Congress of African People (CAP) founding in Atlanta, GA 1970, the Gary National Black Political Convention, 1972, and the National Black Political Assembly (NBA), the African Liberation Support Committee (ALSC), African Liberation Day, the National Black Economic Conferences, National Black United Front,

International Pan African Delegates Reception, and the Black Women United Front.

Akili's involvement at this level exposed him to some of our greatest literary, artistic and political giants of the time, such as James Baldwin, Margaret Walker, Maya Angelou, Jane Cortez, John O. Killens, Sun Ra, Pharoah Sanders, Miriam Makeba, Jamil (H.Rap Brown) Al-Amin, Rob Oba Penny, Mtume, Quincy Troupe, Amina Baraka, Sonia Sanchez, Mohammed Babu, and many others who would have an impact on his political activism and artistic consciousness.

At the end of 1979, Akili returned to the South, organizing in rural Georgia against Klan violence and national oppression. He also served as Chairman of the Wrightsville National Mobilization Committee, Southern Regional Chairman of the National Black United Front, and co-founding member of the Black Fire Poetry Theatre and Black Fire Poets. In 1983, Akili received a Bronze Jubilee nomination for long-term contributor to the arts.

He is currently writing his autobiography, while supporting and serving as an advisor to young activists and writers.

Married to Dr. Né Akili, the couple has three daughters, Ade, Drika and Siyen, one son, Medd and two grandsons, Eli and Sol.

Yaseen A. Assami (Perry W. Davis)

Yaseen Assami was born Perry Wesley Davis on November 12, 1948 in Knoxville, Tennessee. After high school he moved to Cleveland, Ohio.

Here he met several of his long-time friends and Russell Atkins. He, subsequently, became a part of the Muntu Poets. His stay with the Muntu Poets was of short duration but his involvement was very influential and an important part of his development as a youth and a young expressionist writer. Assami counts Russell Atkins as a very good friend and a mentor; a person of unparalleled talent and creative ability. He counts his association with Russell Atkins as an honor. He also has valued relationships with other writers and poets who feel the same esteem for the inspiring literary figure.

Elmer Buford

Elmer Buford was born in Cleveland, Ohio on May 2, 1933. He served in the U.S. Army in Korea and Japan. After his honorable discharge in December, 1955, he took courses at Cuyahoga Community College and Cleveland State University, where he eventually received associate and bachelor degrees respectively.

He authored and published a book named *Conclusions* in 1971 under the pen name B. Felton. Russell Atkins himself wrote the forward for this book. Gaining wide-spread literary recognition, Buford has been published in the *Broadside Press* (Detroit, Michigan), the *Free Lance*, the *Muntu Journal*, the *Sattvas Review*, the *Vindicator,* and other publications.

Robert Fleming

Robert Fleming, a freelance journalist and editor, formerly worked as a writer-consultant with ex-CBS News president Fred Friendly, boss of the legendary Edward R. Morrow for the PBS TV show, Media and Society, after graduating from Columbia University's Journalism school. Employed throughout the 1980s and into the 1990s, he served as a reporter for the *New York Daily News*, earning several honors including a New York Press Club award and a Revson Fellowship in 1990. He worked as a freelance editor and book doctor at Random House's imprint, One World. He taught courses in film and journalism at Manhattan's prestigious The New School. His articles and reviews have appeared in many publications such as *The New York Times, The Washington Post, U.S. News and World Report, Essence, Black Enterprise, Omni, Black Issues Book Review, Quarterly Black Review, and Publishers Weekly*. He has written several non-fiction books such as *Rescuing A Neighborhood, The Success of Caroline Jones Inc., The Wisdom of the Elders, and The African-American Writer's Handbook*. His fiction consists of such works as *Fever In The Blood, Havoc After Dark: Tales of Terror, Gift of Faith, Gift of Truth, and Gift of Revelation*. He edited three anthologies, *After Hours, Intimacy and the Muntu Poets*.

Hzal Anubewei (Anthony Fudge)

Master Poet Hzal Anubewei is his name of enlightenment. His birth name is Anthony Fudge. He was born in Cleveland, Ohio and currently resides in Lithonia, GA. He is a published poet, author, and playwright. He has appeared on radio and tv and was a writer in residence at Albany State in Albany, Ga. He recently completed a mystery novel *Studney and Kilapot* and hopes to publish it along with a book of poetry *Pouring Shade* and a collection of short stories *A Scheme in Every Scene*. His style of poetry has been compared to *Rimbaud* in a 2009 review by Jendi Reiter of Winning Writers. He was one of the founders of *Black Ascensions Magazine* of Tri-C Metro, *The Cleveland Journal,* winning an award from the Cleveland Area Arts Council. He was also published in their first Anthology. He has read with many national poets including Russell Atkins, Norman Jordan, Gwendolyn Brooks, Larry Neal, Amira Baraka, and Nikki Giovanni. As Robert Fleming, a noted New York author once stated, *"Fudge has to write, as necessary as an arm or a leg."* Art Nixon referred to him as "the poets' poet." Owen Dodson after reading his poetry book *The Cry of Beauty* (1976) called him a word – "magician."

Art Nixon

Living in the Los Feliz Village District of Los Angeles, California, Nixon became interested in writing after being introduced to poetry as a member of the Muntu Poets of Cleveland writing workshop headed by Russell Atkins. He wrote and performed his poetry as a member of the Muntu Poets, eventually performing his poetry with various poetry groups locally, at colleges, around the state, and on area radio stations. His interest in writing led him to write essays and poetry for *Black Ascensions* literary and was one of four founders/editors which included Anthony fudge, Larry Howard, and Larry Wade [RIP] in the early 70s. The magazine was a first for Cuyahoga Community College and went on to earn honorable mention for college magazines in *Essence Magazine.*

A Cum Laude Graduate of Case Western Reserve University while married with a 3 year old son, he brought the child to class frequently when babysitters weren't available. [His sin is now a professor at a major Los Angeles University with two award winning books and a third just published, "Race On The QT: Blackness in The Films of Quentin Tarantino," University of Texas Press]. Working to provide for his family, Nixont published papers in Academic Journals as an undergraduate, while employed as a module tutor/instructor at Cuyahoga Community College's writing Lab. He also was employed as a visiting Poet-At-Large for the Cleveland Area Arts Council, introducing Greater Cleveland high school, middle school and elementary students to the first celebrated African American poets as early as 18th century slaves Phyllis Wheatley and Juniper Harmon, the Harlem Renaissance writers to those of contemporary urban poetry.

In Los Angeles, Nixon worked as a security guard for many years while writing screenplays, plays, and TV pilots, none of which he was able to get produced. He also wrote a weekly column for now defunct Las Vegas and Los Angeles black focused newspapers, Bronze News and Balance News for several years. He has been published in several poetry anthologies, including *Black American Literature Forum, The Drumming Between Us, Catch The Fire: A Cross-Generational Anthology of African American Poetry,* and others.

He is included in Columbia Granger's Index of African American Poets. Currently, he is working on the novelization of one of his screenplays. It was published as a short story in Robert Fleming's anthology of short stories, *Too Much Boogie: Erotic Remixes of The Dirty Blues*. He has two sons and two grandkids. He is recently retired as front desk manager at The Beverly Hilton Hotel.

Amir Rashidd

Amir Rashidd was born in Cleveland, Ohio. While residing in Pittsburgh, Pennsylvania, he directed a writers' workshop and taught Black American history (in the oral blues folk tradition) at the Archives Institute of Creative Art. He performed jazz, blues, and poetry on "WYEP" Radio in Pittsburgh.

Rashidd's poetry can be found in several anthologies including Clarence Major's *The New Black Poets* and Quincy Troupes and Rainer Schulte's *Giant Talk* – both published by Random House Publishing. Mr. Rashidd's book, *Sweet Blood Call,* is the first comprehensive collection of Rashidd's work.

Yahya A. Sabur (Jon Hall)

Yahya Abdussabur/nee (Jon Hall) was born August 11, 1943 in Cleveland Ohio. In 1967, after reading the autobiography of Malcolm X and the black nationalist movement, he sought to express this awareness. He was invited to attend a writers' workshop at the opportunities industrialization center, which was located on intersection of Superior Avenue and Ansel Road.

On attending, he was impressed by the black men there and their ability to express themselves by spoken word. He was so impressed that he went home and composed a few poems. This resulted in his being a part of the workshop effort which took the name the Muntu Poets. His membership in the group led to his exposure to a bigger world and to his becoming a devout devotee of Islam that is practiced all over the world.

Mutawaf A. Shaheed (C. E. Shy)

Mutawaf A. Shaheed aka C.E. Shy has been writing since the seventh grade. He continued through high school, until he became more involved in sports. After graduating, he worked at the White Motors Company, where he was involved with the company's newspaper. He started a column called: "the Poets Corner" - which was his first published work.

He moved to Sweden, leaving the "States;" with a one way ticket. He met a Swedish photographer and started writing narratives, accompanying some of the photographs that would be sold to newspapers and magazines.

After returning to the States, he joined a poetry workshop run by Russell Atkins and Norman Jordan from 1966 to 1968. He stopped writing for years, then started back writing again in late 90's; when he started writing novellas and flash fiction, in addition to poetry. Recently, he joined a writing workshop in Cleveland, Ohio in 2011 to hone his writing skills.

Anthology
Volume 2

47 Years Later
With
Russell Atkins